it's not too late

We hope everyday and sometimes don't even recognize it as hope. Using Sitze's field guide will not only make you realize your own hope, but also the hope that surrounds all of us in this world.

Elizabeth O'Loughlin
Stay-at-home Mom
Moscow, Idaho

There he goes again! Bob Sitze talks to me so that things that I thought familiar turn out to be startlingly new. This time it's "Hope." If you plan on breathing tomorrow, you should experience this book today.

Robert Roger Lebel, M.D.
Professor (Genetics), SUNY Upstate Medical University
Syracuse, NY

It's Not *Too Late: A Field Guide to Hope* is a trustworthy compass pointing the way through the wilderness of economic and environmental crises threatening our days. The hope in, with, and through which Sitze writes is not a naive optimism. Rather, it is firmly grounded in the realities of life and faith. Through the use of creative definitions, contemporary quotes, engaging questions, and relevant Scripture passages, Sitze invites and directs the reader to a new, contextual, faith-filled perspective and a hope-filled living. *It's* Not *Too Late* is right on time for these challenging times.

John McCullough-Bade
Pastor and author of *Will I Sing Again? Listening for the Melody of Grace in the Silence of Illness and Loss*
Baton Rouge, Louisiana

While reading this field guide, I doodled "HOPE HAPPENS" in a margin. Hope does indeed happen, for hope is a noun and a verb, as well as a defining adjective for who we are as people of God—hopeful and hope-filled. The selected Bible passages were like comfort food, nourishing the hope that is in me, encouraging me to live in such as way as to make Hope Happen for others.

Emily Demuth Ishida, author
Elmhurst, Illinois

Hope-prophet Bob Sitze delightfully brings to life an ineffable concept. The joyful wisdom in this plucky guide invites us to discover hope, believing we are surrounded by it even in troubling times. Sitze weaves his appreciative and asset-based stewardship understanding throughout these reflections. Like generosity, hope is innate in the human condition, but making either actionable is a choice. Sitze's hope-vocabulary and practical insights will inspire "hopers" living into such choices.

Barbara L. Fullerton, D.Min.
Stewardship Development Program Minister
The United Church of Canada
Toronto, Ontario

As this book makes clear, hope is the foundation of the bold, innovative thinking that our society values so much. Entrepreneurs often survive (and thrive) on little else. If we are to overcome the challenges we face, we need to encourage hopefulness and make it the default attitude for everyone.

Bill Alrich
Account Manager, QAD Inc.
Chicago, Illinois

Study this creative field guide to hope to increase your discernment of hope's power in your life and others. Through this inspiring guide, I walked through the wonders and wisdom of language where hope was unfolded, explained, and expounded upon. It's true, hope clings to me with a fierce and beautiful tenacity, and defines my work as a career counselor and coach to those who are in career transition, unemployed or hopeless about finding meaningful work, even as I experience compassion fatigue. The guide reveals how to use hope-filled tools so that the disprited, anxious and fear-filled among us can once again thrive, even in difficult economic times.

Sandra T. Hagevik, Ph.D.
Career and Executive Coach, Lee Hecht Harrison
Wheat Ridge, Colorado

Compendium, lexicon, vision, testament, manifesto, affirmation, Socratic muse, balm, salve, fertilizer for the soul. All these describe what I*t's* Not *Too Late* is for me as I intuit how my vocation as a writer is also a calling to hope, and how an erstwhile prophet of hope may be reborn!

Lisa Swanson Faleide
Writer, poet, and founder of PlainsSpirit Consulting
Maddock, North Dakota

Teaching is a profession of hope—hope that we can guide and influence others in a positive way. Bob Sitze's field guide helped me to share with my students the science behind "hopeful brains" and how students can strengthen their own hopeful thinking via visualization and self-analysis.

Tim Kaari
Teacher of gifted/talented students
Minneapolis, Minnesota

"Self-help" books have their place. But this book is so much more. It's an artfully drawn map to a kinder future. It's an intelligent guide to the change that you wish to be—and were meant to be—in our troubled world. I especially enjoyed the individual profiles and the "Skills" section, which left me feeling focused, energized, and, yes, full of hope.

Mary Strunk
Associate, Five Colleges Inc.
Amherst, Massachusetts

Curse you, Bob Sitze, you've done it again! You simply will not let me remain the dour cynic that I am naturally inclined to be. And, you've done it in the way you always do, not as a lecturer, but as an engaging conversationalist and a facilitator. You have an aggravating knack for tricking me into participating in a process where you tease truth and hope out of the dark corners of my worldview.

Jay Beech
Baytone Music
Moorhead, Minnesota

"Hope begets hope" is one of the main themes of the conversations that Bob invites us into through his book. Through an 'open source' method, Bob helps us connect with that hope that is inside us and draws on it to engage the sometimes overwhelming issues in our life and world. I was reminded that hope not only lifts us up but is also practical, useful, and effective!

Sunitha Mortha
Director of Global Formation Program,
Evangelical Lutheran Church in America
Chicago, Illinois

Bob Sitze once again puts his own unique interpretation on subjects crucial to us all. His call to face God's world with hope is never more important than today. Hope is not a condition common to most of our approaches to the world. This sense of hope keeps it focused on what God is or can do and away from what we can do to make the world a place resembling God's intention for us. We can never receive too much assistance in order to re-focus our thinking to be more closely with God's will for our lives. Bob does it in ways that aren't threatening and actually makes us laugh at our own silliness.

Gary Brugh
Budget Director, Evangelical Lutheran Church in America
Chicago, Illinois

Hope does exist! We as Christians need to be reminded, and this book does that. It also reminds us that this is not the first economic crisis. We have survived before and we will again.

Anne Zoellner
Executive Assistant, Charles Kitchen Realty
Carson City, Nevada

It's Not Too Late is a superbly timed handbook to support the lagging hope of so many in these economic hard times. Bob uses his breadth of knowledge and his humor to remind us that hope is a gift that should be exercised in reflection, word, and action.

Frank McCann
Peace activist and organizer
Wyckoff, New Jersey

Beyond *A Purpose-Driven Life*, Bob Sitze has written a kind of "Life-Driven Purpose" for our time. In this remarkable, insightful, and fun little book, Bob Sitze shows us how hope lives with each of us, and how we become instruments for hope in the lives of others. Like a daily exercise program for positive, asset-based thinking and action, this book is a treasure trove of gifts in action for anyone and everyone, inside or outside of congregational life.

> Luther K. Snow
> Creator of Asset Mapping and "guru" of good groups.
> Decorah, Iowa

Returning from a week in the dust an rubble of post-earthquake Port Au Prince, Haiti, I landed in the comforting pages of *It's Not Too Late* by Bob Sitze. Observing thousands of international aid workers, soldiers and ordinary Haitians as they struggle to find hope in disaster, the empty void that weighs my soul is calmed by themes of redemption, accountability, attitude, and a hearty call to action in this little book. Perhaps it's not too late for Haiti. Perhaps it's not too late for each of us

> Tim Frakes
> Tim Frakes Productions
> Glen Ellyn, Illinois

It's Not Too Late is a state-of-the-art manual of hope and inspiration. Well written and easy to digest, it contains an arsenal of tools to overcome the despair so common in these times.

> Jonathan Clark
> Mariachi historian
> Livermore, California

it's not too late

it's not too late

a field guide to hope

Bob Sitze

ALBAN

Herndon, Virginia
www.alban.org

The Alban Institute
2121 Cooperative Way, Suite 100
Herndon, VA 20171

Scripture quotations, unless otherwise noted, are from New Revised Standard Version Bible, copyright © 1989 by the Division of Christian Education of the National Council of the Churches of Christ in the United States of America and are used by permission. All rights reserved.

Scripture quotations marked CEV are from the Contemporary English Version of the Bible, copyright © 1991, 1992, 1995 by the American Bible Society, and are used by permission.

Cover design by Crystal Devine

Library of Congress Cataloging-in-Publication Data

Sitze, Bob.
  It's not too late : a field guide to hope / by Bob Sitze.
      p. cm.
  Includes bibliographical references (p. 175).
  ISBN 978-1-56699-397-5
  1. Hope--Religious aspects--Christianity. I. Title.
  BV4638.S55 2010
  234'.25--dc22

                                      2010020472

      10   11   12   13   14   VP   5   4   3   2   1

To my children, Amy, Adam, and Aaron, their spouses, and their children, so that you will always be hopeful people.

Contents

Bogs

Skills

Actions

Connections

Preface

It's never too late for you to hope. Never too late to speak of hope or to act hopefully. Never too late to seek hope. No matter the circumstances in which you find yourself. No matter who wants to tempt you to be afraid, angry, or desperate. These ideas fill this book.

The muse for this book was Hope herself, a quality of Christlike living whose presence is always a sign of God's grace. I've been given hope throughout my life, and in these times of coming ecological and economic decline, I am sure that hope will be an increasingly important gift of God.

For several years I have been following predictions of the almost-certain deterioration of lifestyle quality in the world. I knew that hope might be in short supply, or at least hard to find. I wrote this book to thwart Despair, an ugly demon who wants to nest and rest in our souls, yours and mine. Rather than write yet another book about hope, I thought it best to provide some practical helps for pilgrims who are hungry for hope and want to find it, perhaps like finding Marcus Borg's Jesus, "again for the first time."

I want you to lead others like you—faithful leaders of the people of God—during the difficult times that are surely coming. I want you to be able to follow the example of hopeful people who surround you, invisibly and quietly. I want you to see in God

joy, from Latin, gaudere, "to rejoice"

---

the source of hope who will sustain your spirit and your ministry into the years ahead.

Because hope begets hope, I want your life to be hope-full, so that this precious gift of God's Spirit will not disappear as a motivation for God's people.

May the God of hope fill you with joy.

Where and how will today end for you? How did it begin?

> Rejoice in the Lord always; again I will say, Rejoice.
> —Philippians 4:4

> *The power of hope upon human exertion,*
> *and happiness, is wonderful.*[1]
> *—Abraham Lincoln (1809–1865),*
> *sixteenth U.S. president*

Why a field guide?

You've seen them before, perhaps even used them: little handbooks dedicated to a single purpose, helping you find and appreciate more fully something beautiful, intriguing, and spirit-lifting. "Field guide" is one name for these small, pocketable books that accompany you on an adventure or journey. Field guides help you find something specific, usually within its normal surroundings. Birds, animals, plants, historical artifacts, landmarks—all are described carefully as they exist in their habitat, terrain, or neighborhood. Sometimes a trail or a map graces the field guide, helping make your seeking and finding even more efficient.

This book is a field guide to hope—sized and shaped so that you can carry it along with you on your daily journey of faith. The entries in this book will help you find hope, whether it appears right in front of you or remains elusive despite your searchings.

In the case of this field guide, the "field" is the seemingly inexorable deterioration of the earth's environment and the economic well-being of humankind. Like a handbook about desert plants or inner-city tourism, this book might seem to promote a seemingly futile task: looking for a rare thing amid a hostile environment. In fact, the opposite is true. Just as plants

field, from Old English, folde, "land, earth"

---

bloom in the desert and inner cities teem with barely visible wonderments, so hope flourishes in these difficult years.

This field guide approaches hope-seeking in an appreciative way—believing hope already exists, that it waits your discerning eye and receptive spirit. Because you are looking for hope, you will soon find it to be present all around you—no matter what the field might look like.

With this little pocket book in hand, enjoy the adventure!

What do you call the "fields" in which you live?

The earth is the LORD's and all that is in it,
the world, and those who live in it.
—Psalm 24:1a

No race can prosper until it learns that there is as much dignity in
tilling a field as in writing a poem. It is at the bottom of life we
must begin, and not at the top.[2]
—*Booker T. Washington (1856–1915), U.S. educator*

How to use this book

You've already decided that "hope" is more than just a good idea that all good Christians can agree on, so you have likely set for yourself the requirement to explore hope as a motivating force. (You're probably also *not* reading this book in your favorite rocking chair!)

Because this book is a guide for action, consider these few thoughts about using this field guide to best advantage among those you lead:

- Read the book from start to finish, or skip around inside the entries, choosing titles or ideas that especially appeal to you.
- Keep the book handy as you move through your weekly schedule. Read the entries at different times of day, in different locations, in varied circumstances. This discipline will help make the book useful in a variety of "fields."
- With people you trust, talk about what you read here. Be honest with each other, intellectually and emotionally.
- Use the margins to write notes about your own observations, hints, experiences, or questions.

explore, from Latin explorare, "investigate, search out," perhaps originally a hunter's term, "set up a loud cry" (from *ex*, "out" + *plorare*, "to cry")

- Match up these entries with what you read or see in today's news.
- Connect what you read here with your prayer life.
- Use the entries to shape your confessing, your repenting, your carrying out of your daily ministries in the world.
- Reflect on the thought starters—the word derivations, provocative questions, Bible references, and quotations included with each entry.
- Infuse your journal, blog, Skype, Tweet, or Facebook page with your reactions to the entries in this guide.
- Insert the basic tenets of this book into your daily conversations, relationships, planning, or leadership. And don't confine those activities within the walls of your church.

As you form these entries around your own core convictions, you will shape a more active approach to God's call for your life and a more joyful way of living.

Now, tuck this book into your pocket and purse and get on with your hopeful living!

What would it take for you to consider your life as a hope-filled adventure?

God saw everything that he had made, and indeed,
it was very good.
—Genesis 1:31a

*The good is, like nature, an immense landscape in which man
advances through centuries of exploration.*[3]
*—José Ortega y Gasset (1883–1955),
Spanish essayist, philosopher*

Part 1

Contexts

1   In these times

Because it's a field guide, this little volume starts with entries that look at the "field" itself—the general locations and situations in which you might find the hope you're looking for, or the despair you're trying to avoid. Two simple presumptions guide this section's entries:

- If you don't know where you are, you probably won't be able to figure out where you're going.
- Your contexts shape what you're looking for and how you'll find it.

In this section of the field guide, you'll review what you already know about the times we're in, which can become the fields of hope in which you find yourself. Born as a set of forthright assessments about the currently dire state of the world, this section also pokes holes in that viewpoint, letting some points of light shine on the landscapes you will explore.

In the entries that follow, "in these times" is a phrase into which you can add your own facts, feelings, or fancies. You know your context all too well, so this section presumes that you're savvy about what's happening at this moment in the world's history, especially your own locale. The entries might needle you a bit, injecting into your mind just enough sober reflection to push

context, from Latin *contexere*, "to weave together"

---

your attention and your temperament where they may not want to go.

Be patient with what you read. This Contexts section is just one way this book can help you seek and find hope. Use the margins of the entries to complement what you read there. Insert clippings or notes that add current news items, Web URLs, people to contact, or arguments with what's here. However you use what you read, hear, or experience, make these entries your own.

Enjoy getting to know your surroundings in the readings that follow!

> *"The best of times" and "the worst of times" may*
> *occur at the same times.*
> *—Anonymous*

2   Ignorance is no excuse

If you're finding these times to be overwhelming, you might be tempted to claim that you don't know anyone who's hopeful, as though your lack of knowledge were an excuse to slog around in despair. Even though gloom might seem to fill news stories, undergird advertising, and grab the attention mechanisms of your brain, hope is equally present in those same venues. There's more to know than despair!

Here's an important fact: hope lives large within human societies. In most cultures, it manifests itself as both belief and knowledge. As belief, hope is central to the message of communities of faith. The bedrock beliefs of societies—mostly about God and God's will for the world—are a foundation for their hope. As knowledge, hope comprises propositions that cultures hold about the nature of things, about the process of change, about human existence through the ages. In many societies hope is the prime ingredient for persuasive speech.

Ultimately, hope is an embedded temperament in your brain—a basic approach to all of life—that guides both belief and knowledge. Because a hopeful (or bold and uninhibited) disposition is likely rooted in your genetic makeup, it emerges early in your life. As you mature, hope can become your default approach to life. This happens best when your hopefulness is

ignorance, related to Old Latin *ignarus,* "to be unaware of, not acquainted with"

---

further reinforced by life experiences in which your hopes are realized or rewarded.

Founded in basic humanness, a hopeful approach generates hopeful actions. In your relationships, hopeful actions draw attention and admiration that reinforce their value and utility as a way of approaching life.

Because hope is pervasive and pragmatic in all societies—as actionable belief, knowledge, and temperament—it is hard to claim ignorance of hope's existence or its usefulness.

Unless, of course, you spend all your time watching the despair channels on TV.

For whom might "I don't know how to hope"
actually be true?

Hope is as hope does.
—Anonymous

3 The coming waves

Two large, destructive waves are building or crashing around us, perhaps inside us as well. These crises may seem to be coming upon us suddenly, without warning. These surges of history have become more ominous in our own lifetimes, perhaps because we didn't notice their swelling. Because waves and wavelike occurrences operate according to the laws of physics, we can reasonably predict how these two waves might continue to roll toward the crashing-surf edges of our lives.

The names of the waves are well known: the worldwide economic crisis and environmental collapse. Both waves are likely to continue to influence human history and psychology for the foreseeable future. Both waves could seem to wash away hope, as though despair were actually bedrock.

In the one case—economic collapse—the wave seems to be a relatively short-term occurrence. The collapse of net worth and net profit, a rise in the number of unemployed and underemployed workers, an increase in worldwide poverty, the unraveling of assured economic theory—all point to inevitable outcomes that we hope will be survivable, given time.

In the second case—environmental collapse—the wave is much larger, growing slowly and inexorably, perhaps fueled by the same causes that engendered the first wave. This wave is growing large enough to block our ability to see any reliable reference

collapse, from Latin *collabi,* "to fall or slip together"

---

point for thinking or acting. No human generation has ever experienced the large-scale environmental disaster that has been moving toward us during our mere centuries among earth's eons.

If the great majority of scientists are correct, this wave may not be survivable if we continue to behave as though waves don't exist! On the other hand, we may not survive if we behave as though hope—a wave of God's own creation—doesn't exist!

Perhaps we need to learn to "ride the waves" in new ways?

How do you measure the size of these two waves in your life?

Is not your fear of God your confidence,
and the integrity of your ways your hope?
—Job 4:6

Sea waves are green and wet,
But up from where they die,
Rise others vaster yet,
And those are brown and dry.[1]
—*Robert Frost (1874–1963), American poet*

4 The coming waves (again)

The first wave has probably already crashed into your life. So you may be enmeshed in unhelpful guilt or blaming, or trapped in the paralysis that seeds and nurtures despair. Hope is visible, though, because at least a few world leaders recognize the causes and effects of unbridled greed. They admit their own lack of large-scale and long-term accountability. Now they are working together to resolve these problems.

The second wave severely tests the source, strength, and usefulness of hope. It is possible that you will still be alive when the environment ceases to sustain life for most of the world's population. It seems increasingly apparent that your way of life—a major cause for the wave—will drastically change without your choice. You'll have to change your ways of thinking if you are to survive.

One glimpse of hope: the wave of economic collapse might very well be the dress rehearsal for the second, larger wave. During these times of economic recovery—is this an accurate term for you?—you may be learning together with others how to face the larger wave with tenacious commonality.

Another hopeful sight: although waves cannot be stopped, their effects can be mitigated, their energy dissipated, their force diverted. Complete escape may not be possible, but your

enclave, from Latin *inclavere,* "to shut in, lock up"

---

survivability is enhanced when you remove from the wave the energy it needs to remain powerful and destructive.

One more glance at hope: your influence in these wave-times may be even more powerful than you know. Rather than merely living in a safe enclave or drifting in a well-equipped lifeboat, you have the capacity to gather others toward hopeful attitudes and actions that can bring God's will to bear on what seem to be intractable problems.

Now can you see hope in the waves?

Where else in these waves do you see hope?

[And God said to the sea,]
"Thus far shall you come, and no farther,
and here shall your proud waves be stopped."
—Job 38:11

*Friction (or any opposing force) will eventually reduce the amplitude
of a wave to an undetectable disturbance.*[2]
—Norm Brockmeier

5   We've been here before

Hope can be found in the middle of hopeless circumstance. This truth has always been a biblical theme. As people of God we've been this way before: flooded, surrounded, decimated, and buried. Sometimes clueless, hopeless, and lifeless. Throughout the eons, people just like us have faced dire situations that engendered a continuing prayer—"How long, O LORD?"—as well as continuing laments about our situations.

It's helpful to look back—Scriptures are always a good historical lens—and see how we acted and reacted under duress. Backed up to the sea, ruled by tyrants, weighed down by prosperity, beleaguered by enemies, and overwhelmed by oppressors—those have been the times when our hopes suddenly sprang to life. Songs, poetry, joyful prayers, new visions, surprising leaders, fervor for righteousness—all evidenced God's rescue of us from abysmal conditions.

History is helpful because knowledge of the past can compel actions in similar situations today. Our spiritual ancestors faced down evil; they lived through centuries of corrupt rulers and ruling classes. So have we, and so we will. They paid the price for moral decay, then reformed their cultures. So can we, and so we shall. Like beggars, they faced utter destruction but also experienced God's rescue in miraculous and ordinary ways. So did we, and so we may.

abysmal, from Greek *abyssos,* "without bottom"

We can take heart from the lament of the prophets, the lessons the Babylonian captives learned, the pluckiness of first-century Christians under the boot of Rome, the martyrs, reformers, and missionaries. We can even look at God's most recent history and see how our spiritual parents and grandparents handled economic downturns, wars, and societal upheavals. We don't have to reinvent wheels, ideals, or lifeboats. We have places to turn, stories to retell, examples to follow.

As God's people, we've been here before. Thankfully, so has God!

Where or with whom are you leaving a written record of your own history?

Remember that you were a slave in the land of Egypt, and the LORD your God brought you out from there with a mighty hand and an outstretched arm.
—Deuteronomy 5:15a

History is a vision of God's creation on the move.[3]
—*Arnold J. Toynbee (1889–1975), British historian*

6 Profile: Soul sisters

Sara and Susa are sisters. Both are college students who hope to carve out careers by which they will save the world. They're serious about that goal, and they consider "dietitian" and "social worker" as good ways to achieve that common goal. They understand deeply how much they owe the generations before them, even as they anguish about the sorry state of the environment and its likely effects on their lives.

Depression and avoidance sometimes lurk at the back of their minds. Some of their friends have already given in to the notion that environmental collapse will destroy their lives. Others in their acquaintance have succumbed to generational anger and blaming. And still others won't admit that anything is wrong with hyperconsumptive lifestyles.

Sara and Susa are sticking to larger visions of their lifework. One sees herself eventually becoming involved in "big changes" in the world; the other is content with a smaller version of her life's impact on others. Their parents—and their church—convinced them years ago to be critics of contemporary culture. By their examples, both their parents and their church still support them.

When you talk to these two, they'll tell you that humility is a first step toward their hopeful worldview. They'll talk about not deserving what they have and who they are, about wanting to "pay forward" what has come their way, for the good of the

career, from French, *carriere,* "road or racecourse"

---

world. They see themselves as capable of opening minds around them when those minds aren't already closed by fear, selfishness, or stupidity.

You'd enjoy a conversation with Sara and Susa because, like many of the young adults you know, they are drawn to a life purpose larger than their own happiness. And perhaps some day, when you're about ready to succumb to despair, one of the Saras and Susas who learned hope from you will come back into your life and say thanks.

It's something to hope for, right?

What kind of congregation might Sara and Susa want to be part of? Pray for the soul sisters you know.

All human wisdom is summed up in these two words—
wait and hope.[4]
—Alexandre Dumas (1802–1870),
French writer

7   Much obliged

Obligation: since the sixteenth century, this word has denoted dutiful response to kindness. It's a present- and future-tense word that is also dependent on a past act or relationship. It's a good word to remind you that hope is probably a requirement for your life.

Obligation makes hope necessary. With a strong memory of being favored, you are grateful and thus feel indebted to someone else. You avoid thinking that the world owes you a living, creature comforts, or recognition for your sterling qualities. Because others' kindness or favor gives you hope—and because you are grateful— you want to pass along the kindness (and the hope it engenders) to others.

To state the matter another way: you owe to succeeding generations some measure of hope, some reasons to be hopeful, some hoping skills. Oddly enough, this obligation—to pass hope along—rests on the reality that you can never repay those who made possible your own life. Your only option is to pay forward—to future generations—the debt of gratitude you owe to your forebears. These are the people who loved you, unseen and unknown, as their hoped-for future.

All around you are folk younger than you—children, teens, young adults—whose coming days may be filled with great tribulation. They will likely face degradations of the environment,

oblige, from the Latin *obligare,* "to bind around or up, bind by oath or other tie"

---

lifestyle, and human relations. Their lives will not include the luxuries you may take for granted. They'll want to know that you loved them from the past. They'll want assurance that you tried to accomplish God's will for the world, to bring God's love into the future. They'll want the hope that you offer from the past. And eventually they'll be obliged to pass along hope to the generations that follow them.

Just as you did for them.

Whose future is tied to your hopefulness?

The counsel of the LORD stands forever,
the thoughts of his heart to all generations.
—Psalm 33:11

The future belongs to those who prepare for it today.[5]
—Malcolm X (1925–1965),
American civil rights leader

8 Law and order

In these times, you might also be hopeful because of the law of God. Hope lives inside the law, which infuses the theologies of both the Old and New Testaments. As curb, ruler, and schoolmaster, the law provides you what you cannot invent for yourself, a measure of order in what would otherwise be completely unfettered, destructive selfishness.

One benefit of the law is that it helps engender a civil society, a place where the good of all can be assured. When people agree on the rule of law, disobedience is punished, justice can be applied equally, and law-abiding citizens—those who literally "dwell in the law"—live well together. That's hopeful.

The law also nudges you toward hope-filled repentance. The law invites you to confess that you are by nature a lawbreaker, that you have harmed others and broken your relationship with God. In admitting your wrongdoings, you hope for forgiveness. You become even more hopeful when you vow to amend your totally sinful individualism and trust the power of reconciliation. (Restorative justice is one hopeful example, in which convicted felons turn their lives around because they have been forgiven by their victims.)

The law has another value, to draw you continually toward God. Although you see yourself only as a sinner and a beggar, you hope for something other than continual punishment. Warned,

law, from the Old English *lagu,* "a layer, measure, or stroke laid down"

---

dogged, and even terrorized by the law's dreaded penalties, you see God's grace as a hopeful alternative to saving yourself by imagined total obedience to the law. You can step aside from rampaging self-idolatry and grasp the gift of God's forgiving love.

The delicate-yet-sturdy flower of hope can live within the nurturing soil of the law, a lively and lovely part of your life as a follower of Jesus.

A good thing to remember in these times.

When does the law give you hope?

The law of the LORD is perfect, reviving the soul.
—Psalm 19:7a

The essence of immorality is the tendency to
make an exception of myself.[6]
—Jane Addams (1860–1935),
American social worker

Part 2

Openings

9   Opening and unfolding

Now that you've walked into the fields where hope can be found, you'll need to know what you're looking for. Out here is where you'll find hope in bloom, opening its flowers to show you both its beauty and its eventual usefulness in your life. (Flowers turn into fruit that eventually produces seeds!)

Some of what you read will match what you already know and believe, and some entries may surprise you. Definitions, examples, synonyms, biblical insights, stories, useful descriptors, and side trips—each can help you name the nature of hope.

Part of your hope-finding work is discerning hope from among the lookalikes that you might mistake for hope. (How are hope and optimism different from each other?) Another undertaking: finding what feeds hope and what results from it. (What does resilience have to do with hope? How does hope prosper because of predictable irrationality or thrive despite problems?) This section will help you in those tasks. Another important work for you here: to find the instances where hope has become hybridized with other God-given blessings. (What's the relationship of humility to hopefulness? How do empathy and hope intermingle?) These readings will attempt answers to those questions, too.

This section is a short walk compared to the longer, more intense journey you will continue through life. To learn

bloom, from Old Norse *blomi,* "flower or blossom," and from Old English cognate, *bloma,* "state of greatest beauty"

---

completely how hope unfolds, you will spend the rest of your life examining hope to see what it is, how it works, what happens when it's close at hand. You will seek answers to hard questions— Are hopeful people unaware of reality? What can hopeful people expect of others? How does hope get destroyed? You'll continue to express your gratitude to God that such a thing as hope could exist in the fields of your lifework.

Perhaps "opening and unfolding hope" is your lifework!

When in your life has hope unfolded from bud to flower?

The wilderness and the dry land shall be glad,
the desert shall rejoice and blossom;
like the crocus it shall blossom abundantly,
and rejoice with joy and singing.
—Isaiah 35:1–2a

People stay
Next to the edges of fields, hoping that out of nothing
Something will come, and it does, but what?[1]
—John Ashbery (b. 1927),
American poet

10 Starting with repentance

If hope were a river, one of its sources might very well be the springs of repentance! An odd thought, perhaps, but not an unreasonable one. As a river, hope is deeper and wider than cockeyed optimism. Its flowing within the human spirit probably begins at some smaller spiritual springs. Repentance could be one of them.

Repentance might even be a synonym for hope because, like hope, it latches onto a positive preferred future. If not a synonym, repentance may be a requirement for hope, or perhaps hope's precursor. When you choose repentance, you're less likely to be arrogant or despairing. (Repentant folk have already emptied their souls of the presumptions of self-idolatry.) When you repent, you enter a hopeful, self-sustaining cycle that moves from confession through forgiveness, and then toward living forgiven. (Stopping the cycle at repentance is probably not hope-producing!)

Your decision to repent begins deep within your brain's emotional networks; that's why repentance is a kind of tipping point or trigger that causes you to seek hopeful outcomes. In that way, repentance is a vigorous noun that switches hope from an idea to an action.

Because of the assurance of God's continuing forgiveness, you can repent with confident hope that you will be forgiven by likewise forgiven people around you. (Without God's grace, you'd

slosh, from blending of Middle English *slush* and *slop,* hence "splash about in mud and wet"

---

be foolish to stick out your neck with an admission of wrong-doing, knowing that punishment would instead be the likely outcome!) Because it depends on hope of forgiveness, repentance is a measuring stick for life-sustaining relationships.

For fun, think of the attitudes and behaviors that cluster around repentance: self-reproach, remorse, contrition, willingness to change, regret, ruefulness, grief, discontent. Each word almost gushes with hopeful possibilities for positive change.

Ready to slosh around in repentance?

How does hope flow into your life when you confess your sins?

And if [anyone] sins against you seven times a day,
and turns back to you seven times and says,
"I repent," you must forgive.
—Luke 17:4

Every act of repentance is an act of hope.[2]
—David Heim,
managing editor, The Christian Century

11 Waiting with eager longing

Hope transcends _____. You could put almost any concept, emotion, or situation into that empty space and be writing a statement that's close to universally true. Paul's letter to the Romans illustrates hope's scope. (As an example, see chapter 8:18–27.) For Paul, hope rises above narrowness of mind and spirit, and travels beyond the limits of exclusivity. Hope redeems all of creation—continuously waiting with eager longing for redemption—from the powers of sin and death.

No small matter, hope. Because the entire cosmos is saved by hope, its influence extends past any boundary of class, race, or gender. Because you are joined to creation's own hopefulness, hope drills down deep into your biological core. Because the Spirit herself becomes involved in your prayerful, groan-filled longings, God's own self is wrapped up in your hope. Because freedom and redemption from death's decay are the results of hope, hope is essential to your life—now and eternally.

Hope also counters the futility you experience with all of creation, that you are not going to live forever. Hope reminds you that material possessions will not save you. Because they break, decay, or lose value, your belongings may actually be the root cause of hopelessness. Because of the Spirit's sighs, hope gives you the ability to make words for both your grief and your joy. You pray, you rejoice, you testify, you wait.

transcend, from the Latin, *transcendere,* "to climb over or beyond"

You can derive comfort from the realization that, by choosing to hope, you lay hold of something as large as God's own self. This unobtrusive word stands tall in the gallery of godly attributes, quiet and magnificent. Along with all of creation, you can be patient as your hopefulness gathers strength, as you increase in trust and patience.

Transcendent hope can be at the heart of your eager longings.

When have you experienced prayers too deep for words?

We know that all things work together for good for those who love God, who are called according to his purpose.
—Romans 8:28

The sum of the whole matter is this, that our civilization cannot survive materially unless it be redeemed spiritually.[3]
—Woodrow Wilson (1856–1924),
twenty-eighth U.S. president

12 Mystic, sweet communion

Hope is mystical at its heart, grounded in that centuries-old form of spirituality. Historically, Christian mystics have been hopeful people—few have been known as "grim" and "dour." Like you, they sought a deeper or closer relationship with Christ, and so engaged in spiritual disciplines that would bring them to a fuller understanding of God's nature and God's will for the world.

Wordsmiths from past epochs, wanting to describe people engaged in the act of hoping, went right to *hopeful*. That's because hope tends to fill a person with a quality close to God's own heart. Those ancient word-carvers carried in their souls what you probably feel, too: the need to get closer to God's own Spirit, not to escape the world in despair but to encounter it more assuredly, more joyfully.

For all us mystical-minded folk, hope is probably a literal state of mind. When you hope, your brain likely experiences something unifying—neurobiologists Andrew Newberg, Eugene D'Aquili, and Vince Rause called this phenomenon "absolute unitary being"[4]—that joins you to God and to the entire creation. Hope helps you sidestep fear and its ugly family. Hopeful could be your default way of thinking, even in difficult circumstances.

Another part of the "mystic, sweet communion" that forms the church's one foundation: mystics like you continue to seek because they expect to find. You're patient in that search,

mystic, ultimately from Greek *mystes,*
"one who has been initiated"

---

understanding its lifelong nature. You're insistent that there's
more to life than dying with the most toys. For you, "finding" is
something deeper that connects you with what's truly important.
Hope unites you with others who want to bypass what's
superficial or transient. Hope presents life as both old and new,
something that takes you beyond mindless grasping for meaning.

Gladly, hope binds you to God and God's whole creation.

What words do you use to describe how God's Spirit fills your life?

May the God of hope fill you with all joy and peace in
believing, so that you may abound in hope by the power of
the Holy Spirit.
—Romans 15:13

*Just as in earthly life lovers long for the moment when they are able
to breathe forth their love for each other, to let their souls blend in a
soft whisper, so the mystic longs for the moment when in prayer he
can, as it were, creep into God.*[5]
—*Søren Kierkegaard (1813–1855),*
Danish philosopher

13   Your brain on hope

It might be instructive for you to think about the neurobiology of this most basic characteristic of the human brain. Hopefulness is likely a whole-brain activity—gathering together the workings of a great number of brain structures. Hope is probably a function of your brain's ability to combine various forms of memory with predictive and problem-solving functions in the prefrontal cortex.

On a continuum of basic brain temperaments—large, consistent patterns of feelings—hope is closer to the bold/uninhibited end than to the anxious/inhibited end. The emotions associated with hope may make available the brain's "feel-good" neurotransmitters—such as dopamine, serotonin, and endorphins—that are necessary for optimum decision making and accurate self-awareness.

Hope can be thought of as "an actionable mindset." This means that your brain's abilities to mimic feelings and actions—a function of the amygdala and mirror neurons—likely influence how you think and act positively in daily living. Hopefulness may also be connected to the functions of "the social brain," your brain's ability to discern and act in relationships with others. So you sense or observe hope in others and are thus more likely to think and act hopefully.

Your brain's capacities for memory—including procedural, declarative, and factual memory—may also help equip you to regard

brain, ultimately related to the Greek *bregmos,*
"the front part of the skull"

---

hope as a pragmatic basis for your identity and behavior. Hope may especially determine the character of your emotional memory, the strongest and most long-lasting form of memory in the human brain. (Decisions are first made in the emotional centers of your brain, and only later ratified by the logical, sequential structures.)

Although perhaps not yet within the sharp focus of current brain science, the idea of hopeful brains raises the intriguing question of whether there is a larger, more influential "hope system" embedded in specific brain regions, a foundational capacity given you as a part of God's continuing creation. Whether or not this is true, the basic fact remains accurate: your brain seems wired to hope.

Another evidence that you are fearfully and wonderfully made!

What parts of your brain do you think are hope-filled?

May the God of hope fill you with all joy and peace in
believing, so that you may abound in hope by the power of
the Holy Spirit.—Romans 15:13

Hope is an ability to work for something because it is good.[6]
—Václav Havel (b. 1936), Czech writer and politician

14 Fighting, fleeing, freezing

Fight, flee, or freeze. These are your brain's natural, dependable reactions to fear and stress. They are helpful in many ways but are also eventually destructive of both your brain and the human spirit that lives there—see below. These reactions are understandable—they keep your body safe so that your brain continues to prosper—but they don't leave much room for any kind of hope. They are hardly a way to spend your life with any joy or peace.

Love dissipates cortisol—the brain chemical that accompanies fear-related reactivity and harms essential brain structures and taxes your body's other systems. That's good. The result: hope overrides those first fearful reactions. Although it's no more rational than fear, hope both calms and energizes your brain—your whole brain—for actions that are helpful to more than just your fearful self.

Hope enables you to move past risk-averse thought patterns. It helps motivate you to substitute for the seeming logic of self-preservation another strongly emotional mindset: courage. When you're hopeful, your brain is better able to choose opportunity rather than danger. Hope may help your brain's logical, rational centers reorganize your thought patterns into behaviors that enhance your relationships. When you're hopeful, your brain may have better access to its full potential.

habit, from Latin *habere,* "to have, hold, or possess"

Can you see yourself being hopeful in stressful or fearful situations? Good, because you have that capability if you choose to exercise it. (God chose to create you as a hopeful being, too!) One little problem: If you've become habituated to being fearful, hope may have a harder time breaking through the cortisol-enriched automaticity of fighting, fleeing, and freezing. One little solution: Practice hope as a skill—see the Skills section of this field guide—so that it will also become a habit.

A habit you're starting by using this field guide.

How much are fighting, fleeing, and freezing your habits?

There is no fear in love, but perfect love casts out fear.
—1 John 4:18a

What we fear comes to pass more speedily than what we hope.[7]
—Publius Syrus (first-century BCE),
Latin maxim writer and mime

15   Predictably irrational

Economics is sometimes called the queen of sciences. A usurper has recently shaken the regal fortress of economic theories that have sheltered business and government for decades. This new field of thought is called "behavioral economics," and it offers hope to what some have also termed "the most dismal science."

In the dusty past, economic theories were based on trust that most people were capable of making rational decisions about their lives. "Enlightened self-interest" is the catchphrase that describes this way of thinking. Behavioral economists—Dan Ariely and Bill McKibben, for example—have challenged bedrock economic theory with experimental evidence that shows decision making to be largely irrational. (People buy what isn't good for them, overspend and undersave, cheat, lie, and steal without logic.) It seems that decision making about matters of economic well-being might be a hopelessly chaotic activity within the human psyche.

The results of a variety of experiments suggest that the irrationality is actually predictable! In other words, choices that don't make good sense seem to occur in patterns that can be expected with some degree of certainty. This new view of economic behaviors—at the center of our living and thinking— now seems hopeful.

If we can finally understand the bases upon which decisions are made, irrational or not, we can understand better how we

enlighten, from the Old English *inlihtan,* "to remove the [figurative] dimness or blindness from one's eyes or heart"

---

think, and can better counteract what isn't working. It's hopeful to admit the truth about human nature and to know where people need help. We can deal with people as they really are, irrational warts and all, and approach matters such as simplicity, generosity, and hyperindividualism with increased wisdom.

And if we no longer believe that rationality is at the heart of this queenly science, perhaps we will come to rely instead on hopeful, predictable irrationality.

Which would really be in our self-interest—right?

In what ways do your decisions sometimes defy reasonable explanations?

For the love of money is a root of all kinds of evil.
—1 Timothy 6:10a

Money is probably the most costly way to motivate people.[8]
—Dan Ariely (b. 1968), Israeli-American behavioral economist

The irrationality of a thing is no argument against its existence, rather a condition of it.[9]
—Friedrich Nietzsche (1844–1900),
German philosopher, classical scholar, critic of culture

16   Hope as wisdom as hope

Saps and sages alike seek wisdom; it's been that way for eons. Ancient and not-so-ancient societies have dug in the fertile bed of wisdom, hoping to enrich their cultures with its quality. (Most recently, a group of researchers at the University of Chicago's DEFINING WISDOM Research Network Project [See http://wisdomresearch.org] have begun adding scientific language to this highly desired human trait.)

In your life, hope and wisdom probably keep company with each other. At difficult times you may have mistaken one for the other. Why is that? Both wisdom and hope come to you only after years of experience or thought. Both are actionable mindsets in your brain; both deal with desirable futures based on careful distillation of past experiences. Both call out of your psyche what most people would call the best in human nature. Both might help you transcend the traps of automatically reactive thought and behavior. And both can have a spiritual component that anchors them.

Are all wise people hopeful? No. Neither are all hopeful people wise. Fools can hope, and wise people can despair. For most of us, though, these two qualities seem to be combined in our day-to-day approaches to life.

Why note this twinning of two human attributes? To observe that in seeking one, you may find the other. Or,

sap, ultimately from the Latin, *sapere,*
"to taste, have taste, be wise"

---

conversely, that in losing one you may inadvertently let go of the other. As you notice either quality taking root in your spirit, you can also see how the attributes of the other might be gathering around you.

Like everyone else, you'll probably never be completely wise or hopeful. Don't let this deter you from seeking both hope and wisdom. In some ways, that quest may be the most deeply satisfying way to carry on your life's journey.

May you travel the ancient roads with joy!

When do you find yourself especially hopeful-and-wise together?

If any of you is lacking in wisdom, ask God, who gives to all generously and ungrudgingly, and it will be given you.
—James 1:5

Web pages with WISDOM *in their content: 311,000,000.*
Web pages with HOPE *in their content: 2,147,483,647.*

17 Profile: The pastor with (no) problems

Jaylene's a pastor with problems. To look at her, you'd never guess that this attractive person with an effervescent personality would be carrying around more personal predicaments than the CEO of a bankrupt corporation. But have a conversation with Jaylene, and you'll soon understand the turmoil she lives with each day.

For starters, there's the former husband who wants to embarrass her in front of her congregation, the mountain of debts he incurred on their joint bank and credit-card accounts, the home she can't sell, the car that doesn't want to run consistently, and a severe economic depression in her locale.

Add to that her congregation, split wide open when her long-term pastor predecessor retired early to begin another career in the same community. Lately Jaylene's physical health has been playing tricks on her—she knows about stress—and some days she's not sure about her mental stability, either.

If you talk long enough with Jaylene, though, you get the strong feeling that she understands and lives hope. Even with problems buffeting her on all sides, Jaylene still knows how to turn her emotional and spiritual sails to catch the wind of the Spirit. Her judicatory has assigned an experienced mentor to her, the church members shower her with empathy, and Jaylene knows that her assets as pastor are an exact fit for the opportunities embodied in this congregation.

problem, from Greek *proballein,* "to throw forward"

In all her dilemmas, Jaylene does not think of herself as riddled with difficulty or as a person identified by her problems. Instead, she gathers about herself her strong sense of calling, the congregation's exciting assets, and her trust in God's providence— and keeps working at hopeful living. Seeing even her problems as useful, she's whittling the mountain of her troubles down to the size of a molehill.

This hope thing? Jaylene gets it.

In what ways are you part of your pastor's hopefulness?

Do your best to present yourself to God as one approved by him, a worker who has no need to be ashamed, rightly explaining the word of truth.
—2 Timothy 2:15

The Christian resolution to find the world ugly and bad has made the world ugly and bad.[10]
—Friedrich Nietzsche

18 What's "God's abundance," anyhow?

Just a few months ago, it seemed easy for Jorge to define "God's abundance." A woodworking artisan with a steady clientele, Jorge had always been grateful for "an abundant God who gives us more than enough." He felt comfortable—and even worshipful—approaching God with humility. He also harbored just a little twist of guilt about his good fortunes.

In a faltering economy though, that understanding of abundance seems strangely out of place. No Sundays-only Christian, Jorge knows that claiming more-than-enough abundance as God's will is either intellectual dishonesty or the Prosperity Gospel run amok. Because a significant number of people at his church have crashed over a financial cliff, the habit of invoking "the God who wants you to have more" now leaves Jorge feeling empty.

How have Jorge and those like him shifted their understanding of "God's abundance"? By reassessing the place of "more" in their lives and by valuing "enough" more highly. They're discarding the "plentiful possessions" and "overflowing pleasure" meanings of abundance. They're moving from needless to needful wants. They're replacing self-gratification with self-emptying. They're not obsessing about new scarcities, instead delighting in new "luxuries." They're focusing on their

abundance, from the Latin *abundāre,*
likely rooted in "flowing water"

---

sufficiencies and capabilities, using what they already have to get God's will done in the world.

In your life, this change is not accomplished with the wave of a rhetorical wand. This shift in attitudes and behaviors can take place within the relationships that already exist and will emerge within your community of faith. In heartfelt conversation and shared experiences, the people of this congregation and you can help each other sort through the mess of your mixed emotions and find courage to live with a sense of sufficiency!

In these times, your views of an abundant God can equip you to live life fully, with joy and generosity. Jorge will be right there, too.

Where in your spiritual life does "God wants you to be rich" still linger? Why?

If we have food and clothing, we will be content with these.
—1 Timothy 6:8

In case you haven't noticed, "more" doesn't work anymore.
—Anonymous

19 Empathy and hope

Hope doesn't do well when it stays inside just you. To be an effective world-changing force, hope has to spread beyond the boundaries of your own feelings. Your hopefulness unfolds its full potential when it reaches beyond your private attitudes and actions, when it gathers others' hopefulness alongside your own. (See the Connections section for more on this idea.)

That's where empathy enters. Empathy is an appreciative knowledge of others' situations, their emotions, their intentions for what's yet to come. It's an intuitive way of walking in others' shoes. Empathy is probably also a two-way street: You see and understand yourself in me, just as I know myself because of what I see in you. So you and I can be hopeful together because we recognize and value hope in each other.

Hope is taught, studied, and proclaimed, but it's also caught, discovered, and experienced. You and I don't force-feed each other our particular brand of hopefulness. We don't squeeze it out of each other, either. Because you and I are empathetic, we recognize our potentially hopeful selves in each other, and call out of each other the hope that God has placed there. In this way, empathy adds power to hope.

Empathy is also powerful because it can engender courage; I see hope in you and so am emboldened to cast aside my reluctance or timidity in difficult circumstances. Your example

empathy, from Greek *empatheia,* "in passion"

---

helps me discover that I'm not the only one who is hopeful. I find strength in that truth. Empathy is effective because neither you nor I want to let down each other. As it spreads beyond just the two of us, empathy helps groups of like-minded people gather together in mutual appreciation, in concerted action.

Now can you see why empathy works so well alongside hope?

What does it take for you to show empathy? To receive it from others?

In everything do to others as you would have them do to you.
—Matthew 7:12a

Whatever can happen to anyone can happen to me.[11]
—*Muriel Rukeyser (1913–1980), American poet*

20 Resilience

It's always fun to notice new buzzwords. One expression in the current crop is *resilience*. In present parlance, resilience implies a plucky sturdiness of the human spirit. "We're resilient, so we don't crumble like cookies in the face of difficulty." Or, "We are resilient, so we bounce back when buffeted by disappointment." Hope seems to leap out of resiliency the way delight springs out of children on a playground.

While appreciating any words that bring hope into focus, we field-guide wordsmiths also carry the duty of looking critically at the way words are used. In this case, please permit this caution: Don't pounce on *resilience* just yet. Why? It may not be that hopeful.

At its root, the word denotes the capacity of anything to return to its original state. When applied to people, that resilience is admirable, but it may be less than helpful. Going back to one's original state of being, ways of behaving, or identity may be the least hopeful way to behave in these times. Ask yourself this question: Why would you or anyone else want to spring back to the ways of thinking and behaving that got you into this mess in the first place? Another question: What makes you so sure that your basic temperament—the place you're bouncing back to—is helpful or hopeful?

adroit (dexterous), perhaps corrupted from French phrase *á droit,* "according to right"; eventually from Latin *directum,* "right, justice"

It is certainly a good thing that you can't be knocked over permanently, that you keep coming back, that you hold to your original intentions for a godly life. But where in *resilience* is the flexibility that allows for your new shape, size, direction, or identity? Could you, the hopeful person, also be nimble, adaptable, or adroit without ever going back to your starting place?

Or should we wordsmiths just find other, newer words to describe you?

How might you find your "original state"?

Therefore, my beloved, be steadfast, immovable, always excelling in the work of the Lord, because you know that in the Lord your labor is not in vain.
—1 Corinthians 15:58

The beginning of wisdom is to call things by their right names.
—*Chinese proverb*

21 Epistemological modesty

Conservative newspaper columnist and political commentator David Brooks recommends that we take on "epistemological modesty" in the face of a world overrun with information and knowledge but short on wisdom. Brooks's basic idea: You can never completely know or understand the complexities of life, so you should be modest about your abilities to deal with them wisely. Brooks surfaces another, related question: Would you do better to trust your spiritual core in matters beyond your understanding?

You might be in that situation right now:

- The standards for your long-range strategic plans don't seem to measure meaningful outcomes as well as you anticipated.
- The evidence of your success continues to disappear into the dust created by downwardly mobile investments.
- Regardless of national diplomacy, entire countries still behave in ways that defy logic.
- A significant number of societal institutions around you seem inept or feckless.

Brooks's thoughts might help you understand the value of hope. When you admit your inability to understand completely what is happening in your life, epistemological modesty seems a likely result. Hope could take the place of any false notions about

modesty, from Latin *modestus,* "keeping measure, moderate, sober"; **epistemology,** from the Greek *epistasthai,* "knowing how to do, understand"

---

your knowing everything. Hope could help you interpret your life more realistically and provide motivation for change that isn't rooted in impossibility.

At this moment in your personal history you might be most right and righteous to rely on hopefulness nested inside epistemological modesty. Why? Faking your self-confidence doesn't fool anyone, so hope can provide you a pragmatic alternative. Tinged with modesty and humility, hope can replace self-idolatry and join you with others in relationships that are intellectually and emotionally honest. You can face down the complexities of these times, admit your shortcomings, and draw on the wisdom and capacities of other equally modest epistemologists.

And also use smaller words to describe grander possibilities!

In what parts of your life are you feigning comprehension or expertise?

[Do not] think of yourself more highly than you ought to think, but . . . think with sober judgment.
—Romans 12:3

22   Hope is slow

In a fast-paced, rabbits-win-the-prize world, it might not give you comfort to know that hope is slow. Yes, slow. Because hope is a whole-brain activity, the neurons that create hope can take longer to get together as a thought. In fearful circumstances, hope is not the default reaction, and so must wait for fear to subside.

If hope is outside your experience or capacity at the moment, you must rely on others to help you find the hope hiding inside you. That reliance delays hope's arrival on your attitudinal doorstep. Because hope connects past experiences, present contexts, and positive outcomes, your brain takes awhile to apprehend hopefulness. And deciding to act on hope? Acting on hope takes even longer, because all the decision making and motor circuits in your brain have to coordinate their neuronal firings so that you can act on your hope.

Slow isn't always bad, though. Yes, sometimes turtles win races. Slow can also suggest careful consideration, delicate cooking that preserves quality, the thorough spread of something, and outcomes that are less prone to mistakes or hasty judgments. When you're looking for hope, these are probably desirable behaviors.

In your own life, slow might also mean "taking life at a manageable speed," always a hopeful approach. Slow might imply

fast, from Old English *fæst,* "firmly, strongly, vigorously"

---

leisure, self-restraint, or lack of pressure. Slow might be better for your relationships, your physical well-being, your spiritual health.

How might you react to the slowness of hopefulness? First, wait patiently for hope to appear. Second, wait with assurance that hope will benefit your life. (If, while waiting, you have any doubts about slow hope, think how well fast is working for you!) Third, when hope arrives, greet it with reverence, relish its appearance, and hold onto it dearly.

You might also avoid rabbits with winning smiles.

In what ways has hope been slow to come into your life?

> So do not worry about tomorrow, for tomorrow
> will bring worries of its own.
> —Matthew 6:34a

> *Better to wait for a chicken dinner than to*
> *grab a chicken on the run.*
> *—Anonymous*

23   Tiny holes in reality

Reality is sometimes used to name the barriers that might impede any kind of positive change. Ever had this happen to you? "Well, Amery, you might want to turn the church's front lawn into a garden, but the reality is that _____." In citing reality, people who are fearful or despairing probably misconstrue what is actually true, right, or beautiful. Out of their own hopelessness, they take away from hope its ability to motivate action.

One thing you should know about hope: it breaks through reality. Why? Although reality might look like an impermeable blanket of negative facts, it's filled with holes!

You can't see them until you get really close, but they're there, little imperfections in any negative outlook about factual matters. In fact, reality is variegated in its texture and composition, thin and vulnerable. Reality is marked with multitudes of holes—in its logic, its effects, or its accuracy.

Those are places where spiritual truths—faith, love, forgiveness, empathy, generosity—find those holes in the supposedly impregnable outer layers of reality. Hope is also one of those spiritual truths; it finds and expands the holes in negative perceptions of life. That capacity of hope starts with probing questions—"How do you know that?" "What's bound to change, anyhow?" "Is that still true in these times?" or "Why should I believe that anymore?" Eventually a hopeful person

reality, from Latin root, *realis,* "real existence,"
originally a legal term in the sense of "fixed property"

---

comes through to the other side of "reality," like a traveler who
has passed through to the other side of a thunderstorm and sees
a beautiful sunlit cloud mass. That's where you can be, once you
don't let "reality" become a barrier to your own hopefulness, once
you don't let despair get to name what's true.

Because there are hopeful holes in reality, you can see your
way through!

When has hope helped you see or pass through "reality"?

Whoever observes the wind will not sow;
and whoever regards the clouds will not reap.
—Ecclesiastes 11:4

To be realistic today is to be visionary.
To be realistic is to be starry-eyed.[12]
—Hubert H. Humphrey (1911–1978),
U.S. vice president, 1965–1969

Part 3

Bogs

24 Beyond first appearances

Finding hope isn't necessarily a trip through a field of posies. Along the way you're likely to run into squishy bogs that slow down your exploration for hope. Like the rest of a godly life, hope-seeking is likely to include moments when you suddenly realize that what you're doing is more difficult than you first imagined.

In this section of *It's Not Too Late*, you will encounter the quagmires that might keep you from being hope-filled. Not an exposé or an unmasking, these entries instead take you behind the scenes to examine these barriers respectfully. As you know what can get in the way of being hopeful, you'll be better able to slog around, over, or through those barriers. Perhaps you'll learn how to avoid the paths that lead into bogs.

In these entries you may also find some ways in which hope can get dinged and scratched like a car door in a parking lot. These readings may help you acknowledge those blemishes, too. Don't be discouraged by what you find. As you have probably discovered in your own less-than-perfect life, when you finally get a little closer to what's not gleaming brightly, what's not flawless and faultless—that's when you start to see the true beauty of what's standing in front of you. The flaws and the flecks of imperfection can turn out to be distinctive marks of character, useful and attractive in their own way!

bog, from Gaelic and Irish adjective *bog,* "soft and moist"

Add your own comments and questions that help you slosh through the bogs or cover the blotches. In that way, when you're finished with this section you may find hope to be even more approachable, more desirable. Perhaps you'll even come to relish the prospect of being a hopeful steward of God's love for the world.

A pleasant possibility, indeed!

What gets in the way of your hopefulness?

[The LORD] drew me up from the desolate pit,
    out of the miry bog.
      —Psalm 40:2a

Those who wish to sing always find a song.
    —Swedish proverb

25 Who wins, who loses

In these times of slow economic and ecological collapse, there seem to be both winners and losers. Predictably enough, the winners are the elite—including the religious elite—who may play economic games more efficiently than the losers. The losers are poor people, whose lives and lifestyles deteriorate more quickly. Fueled by populist rage or worse, the losers eventually turn on the winners, and class warfare breaks out. The winners have to work harder at holding together "the good life" and eventually succumb to the power of the larger number of losers.

As you come to grips with the world's increasingly desperate condition, you might see signs such as these that indicate the tension between winners and losers:

- Rampant individualism, perhaps legitimated by the church and its theologies
- Increasing numbers of gated communities and private security firms
- Sprawling, mutually exclusive ghettos of the rich and the poor
- The beginnings of anarchy, or the breakdown of civility
- Institutions—such as the church—that don't work very well

When despair about life's diminishing qualities reaches a critical mass, people lose because they forsake their best selves.

win, from the Old English expressions *winnan,* "struggle for, work at, strive, fight" and *gewinnan,* "to gain or succeed by struggling"

Simply to survive, desperate people discard generosity, selflessness, patience, or tolerance. As they respond to extreme stress, despairing people fight, flee, or freeze. Eventually they lose their will and ability to work together. The church loses, too, if its message of hope seems to lack significance or power in these most important matters. Despair creates people whose attitude spreads virally, creating a cycle of desperation that threatens to drown the civilization.

As they are drawn down into whirlpools of loss, desperate people create the harsh consequences of an attitude that besmirches them individually and tarnishes the image of God given to all people in creation.

Not the win-win God had in mind.

Who first thought of winning as better than "losing"?

In the day of prosperity be joyful, and in the day of adversity consider; God has made the one as well as the other.
— Ecclesiastes 7:14a

My Jesus Mercy[1]
—epitaph on gravestone of Alphonse Gabriel "Al" Capone
(1899–1947), American gangster

26   Living at the edges

Despair-avoidance is one of the swamps where your hope might get mired. This attitude is based on the idea that any negative feelings—despair being one of them—destroy any possibility of acting in a hopeful way. In this frame of mind, you might consider hope and despair to be complete opposites of each other.

But what if hope is never far from despair? What if they are so close that they share some of the same characteristics? What if, to be hopeful, you need sometimes to admit your despair? In that case, you might discover that both hope and despair

- are "high emotions," involving large sections of your brain;
- compel some kind of response or action;
- can become habitual;
- sharpen each other. (Without despair, hope might become insipid; without hope, despair could turn you into a joyless prune.)

When you live at the edges, you allow both hope and despair to reside in your mind, holding both approaches to life in tension. You admit that both hope and despair can motivate your spirit. When you live at the edges between hope and despair, you don't try to dodge despair. Instead, you see this situation as an opportunity to grow stronger, bolder, or wiser. To strengthen

profound, from Latin *profundus,* "deep, bottomless, vast"

---

hope, you take the risk that profound hopefulness might suddenly teeter in the direction of deepening despair. In edge-living you participate in the abundance God gives, risking failure or death. You ferret out opportunities from what appears hopeless. You tilt toward hope even as you acknowledge the presence and power of despair. You remain close to people stuck in despair, ready to invite and assist them out of their quagmire.

And you depend on the Spirit to hold you safely at the edges of life.

Where in your life do you live close to the edges between hope and despair?

Out of the depths I cry to you, O Lord.
Lord, hear my voice!
—Psalm 130:1

What reinforcement we may gain from hope; if not, what resolution from despair.[2]
—John Milton (1608–1674), English poet

27 Lies we believe

Satan's trickery likely includes a set of beguiling lies about the existence or effectiveness of hope. Satan is full of believable baloney that's just persuasive enough to tempt your spirits away from hopefulness. Exposed, these falsehoods drop their smirking masks and lose their power. Here are a few of those lies; perhaps their exposure here will keep hope from leaking out of your soul:

- Grabbing for what you can get works better than hoping to receive it.
- There's no reason to hope if "more" isn't possible.
- Don't hope for cooperation or collegiality; you have enemies everywhere.
- You deserve what you have or get; hope just makes you into a beggar.
- Don't hope for the best in other people; survival of the fittest still works.
- Hope is the province of people with small minds and weak bodies.
- Don't put your hope in any institution of society, especially government of any kind.
- Hope distracts you from now. Now is more important than later.
- To realize your hopes, require quantifiable proof.
- There's only one way to be strong; being hopeful isn't it.

proof, from Latin *probare,* "to test, prove worthy" (ultimately from *probus,* "worthy, good, upright, virtuous")

- Here's something you can count on: you earn what you get, and you make your own breaks.
- Because shortcuts and quick fixes work well, keep your hopes small.
- It's too late now to hope that civilization can avert coming economic and ecological disasters.

Add to this list other lies that you have experienced. That way you won't ever be fooled by Satan or his devilish co-conspirators into thinking that hope is unreal, unworkable, or unwieldy. By naming ideas that weaken hope, you can sharpen your vision and fortify yourself against the falsehood that hope isn't a valuable part of your life.

After all, there's nothing tricky about hope.

What seeming truths about hope might actually diminish your hopefulness?

Even Satan disguises himself as an angel of light.
—2 Corinthians 11:14b

Every thing that is done in the world is done by hope.[3]
—Martin Luther (1483–1546),
campus pastor and reformer

28   Profile: Posh and piffle

Geoffrey's been a church guy for most of his life. Even though he's a young adult, he buys the idea of organized religion. He has elected not to follow the majority of his age cohort in the false choice of rejecting religion in favor of spirituality. Lately, though, Geoffrey has been rethinking his loyalties and what's behind them.

In the middle of a continually deteriorating economy and environment, some religious leaders Geoffrey respects have been preaching and saying things that just don't square up with what Geoffrey knows to be true. "We've already come past the intersection of hope and fear," says one. "As Christ's followers, we are always people of hope." Another keeps harping about "the victory we have in being Easter People," even while his denomination is losing members and funding faster than gravy escapes mashed potatoes. Still another national leader is certain that "God's rescue will come upon us, as of old," as though scientific prognostications about the environment were reversible by prayers or miracles.

Geoffrey's loyal, but he is not easily tempted to check his brains at the door of the church's pronouncements. Lately he's been asking more difficult questions about the places where faith, science, economics, and politics meet. He's been poking at his denomination's positions on the environment and noticing where rampant individualism is still legitimated in some bully pulpits.

posh and piffle, unknown origin; an expression meaning "lacking substance"

He's been looking for the places in organized religion where in-depth analysis and in-your-face actions could replace shallow thinking and token activism. He's insisting on intellectual honesty in his faith community.

Geoffrey's own pastor is right there with him, asking the same questions, searching Scripture, praying without posturing, wrestling with God's will for the congregation, and helping Geoffrey hold onto hope.

Even in the face of religious posh and piffle.

How do some religious utterances evolve into empty expressions?

Then I said, "Ah, Lord God! Here are the prophets saying to them, 'You shall not see the sword, nor shall you have famine, but I will give you true peace in this place.'" And the LORD said to me: "The prophets are prophesying lies in my name; I did not send them, nor did I command them or speak to them."
—Jeremiah 14:13–14

A lie is an abomination to the LORD,
and a very present help in trouble.
—Anonymous combination of Proverbs 12:22 and Psalm 46:1.

29   Fundamental terror

Hope helps you to be accepting, welcoming, and flexible. That's one of the reasons why it may not fit with the persuasive rhetorical flourishes of both fundamentalism and terrorism. Both "isms" make statements about what is wrong and right, with the differences between them portrayed in stark terms. While hope draws pictures of the world in terms of "we," fundamentalism and terrorism frame their worldview with "them against us." (Remember that although fundamentalism and terrorism may be similar, they are not the same. To say this another way, many terrorists are fundamentalists, but few fundamentalists become terrorists.)

Because these two ways of thinking are rigid, they can impede the flow of life-freeing motivation that comes from hope. If you believe the premises of either fundamentalism or terrorism, you might not need hope, because the outcomes you desire result instead from your obedience to bedrock principles. Hope may not seem as righteous as other fundamental beliefs, and it may not appear as effective in accomplishing what you desire. Hope might even weaken your power to change or defeat your enemies.

If you have accepted the precepts of fundamentalism or terrorism, you may have already forsaken hope as a legitimate way to think and act. And having relinquished hopeful behaviors,

terrorism, from "terrorize," to coerce or deter by terror; ultimately from Latin *terrere,* "to fill with fear, frighten"

---

you may also have accepted either fundamentalism or terrorism as your preferred core identity. There may be little room in your brain for hope.

Once the guiding principles of terrorism or fundamentalism become habituated, they are not easily reversed or gentled. Like hopefulness, they create their own system of self-justifying proofs. They feed, perpetuate, and legitimate themselves. They can create barriers that wall out the rest of the world.

One more thing: Because Jesus was accepting, welcoming, and flexible, he was probably not a fundamentalist or a terrorist. Instead, he was hopeful.

> **Why might some people be attracted to fundamentalism or terrorism as legitimate ways for changing the world?**

> But I say to you, Love your enemies.
> —Matthew 5:44a

> *Everyone knows scientists insist on using complex terminology to make it harder for True Christians to refute their claims.*
> *—Entry in fundamentalist chat room*

30   Aphasia and ineffability

Hope depends on words for its power. "No words, no thoughts."
So goes the psycholinguistic maxim that establishes the
importance of words. A lack of words about hope results in a
lack of hopeful thoughts. Another place where hope gets
bogged down.

If you don't have enough brain power to retrieve or use
words, you suffer from aphasia. Most aphasia is related to brain
damage—disease and dementia come to mind here. It is also likely
that at times of high emotion—fear, anger, sorrow, despair— you
might experience a momentary or drawn-out aphasia. Words
escape you, or at least seem as though they're hiding from you for
those moments.

Another kind of inexpressibility comes from the profundity
of the experience. From time to time you may have been unable
to express yourself because of the enormousness or implications
of an experience. Your vocabulary or sentence-making abilities
just weren't up to the task of defining, describing, or sharing what
had just taken place. The experience was ineffable, literally beyond
words. Your attempts to describe your thoughts seemed trivial
when compared to the intensity of the moment. (Think of first
love or a "mountaintop experience.")

At its core, hope is probably ineffable. You cannot easily
express its nature, its reach into your life, its hold on your

aphasia, from the Greek *aphasis,* "without utterance"

---

emotions. And yet, as with all feelings, it depends on words to gather together sections of your brain for action. Without a practiced lexicon of hope, you may not be able to influence others. Without frequent expression, your brain may sequester hope in one of the back corners of its memory. ("Use it or lose it" may literally describe this phenomenon.) The solution? Find and learn a "hope vocabulary" as soon as possible. Then teach it to others!

This field guide might help.

How could you strengthen your ability to express your hopefulness?

Woe is me! I am lost, for I am a man of unclean lips, and I live among a people of unclean lips; yet my eyes have seen the King, the LORD of hosts!
—Isaiah 6:5

May the Baby Jesus blow your mind and shut your mouth.
—1960s-era Christmas card

31   Mice that don't run away

Your hope can get bogged down when you can't tell the difference between causes and effects, or when life's usual vagaries become more erratic or uncontrollable. Neurobiologists have learned this from mice.

Given the right circumstances—electrical shock—mice behave predictably: they run away from the shock or stop engaging in the behavior that has, in their little rodent minds, caused the shock. When the going gets tough, tough mice get going.

But subject mice to seemingly random jolts of electricity— with no connection between cause and effect—and over time those same mice will not run away. Lacking control of the perceived cause of their distress, shocked mice stand or sit in the same place, as though they have given up. In experiments over thirty years, this behavior—or nonbehavior—has been dubbed "learned helplessness." Levels of chemicals essential for brain function are reduced significantly, resulting in forgetfulness and a decline in mental focus. Not good for brains of any kind or size.

It would be presumptuous to say that the mice, intelligent as they are, stopped being hopeful. But if you were subjected to the same unpredictable, stressful conditions—"shocked" in different ways—your reactions could be described as learned helplessness. And when you have become helpless, you have also learned to

random, from Old French *randon,* "rush, disorder,
impetuosity, force"; ultimately from randir, "to run fast"

---

be hopeless. Your behavior may seem like complacency or apathy,
but it may also be a rational reaction to continuing stress. The
logical, sequential parts of your brain do what your emotional
self requires. Other mindsets—discouragement, a sense of futility,
depression—soon gather around your helplessness as happy, non-
stressed mice congregate around cheese.

The antidote to learned helplessness? Learned mastery,
learned optimism, hardiness, and experiences in which you learn
what you can control and what you cannot.

You can thank mice for this bit of hope.

In what areas of life have you learned to be helpless?

So let us not grow weary in doing what is right.
—Galatians 6:9a

*Wishful thinking is not a sufficient strategy
when nothing makes sense.*
—Anonymous

32   Who and what saves us?

In end-of-the-world-as-we-know-it literature, the jury is still
out about who or what can save us from the great tribulations
its proponents believe are coming this way. On the one hand,
some writers are certain that we can still fix the problems—as
we have in the past—with technological solutions. In their view,
if technologies got us into this mess (think internal combustion
engine) then improved technologies can get us out—think
electric cars. Other writers, who propose a new world order, tend
to think that the perpetually ugly wounds in the human condition
can be healed primarily by profound changes in attitudes,
especially as we gather together in communities of action. Think
"coming to the same mind."

Both approaches are hopeful about the efficacy of human
effort when it's focused on a specific problem or condition.
Both ways of thinking leave open a small entry portal where
theocentric spirituality can have a strong influence. Both
approaches call for nearly universal changes in attitude and
priorities within societies. Both use urgency and love of humanity
to motivate others.

Unfortunately, both options also hold open a large door for
self-idolatry. Grand visions of salvation from the coming calamities
could rest squarely on the idea that we can harness the power of
the (seriously flawed) human spirit. Technologies could become

technology, from Greek *tekhnologia,* "systematic treatment of an art, craft, or technique," originally referring to grammar

---

Babel-like, creating overloads of magnificent information and artifacts but also siphoning off large amounts of attention, energy, time, money, and other resources. Technological fixes could tempt us to abandon today's compact fluorescent light bulbs and hybrid cars and to embrace tomorrow's supposedly sure-fire solutions. These approaches to changes in the human spirit could easily be derailed by blind optimism or overactive trust in human nature.

In the final analysis, we don't save ourselves. Not individually, collectively, or technologically. Individually, collectively, and surrounded by our technologies, we're just not big enough, smart enough, selfless enough to save ourselves.

Something else, someone else may be our only real hope.

> Those who try to make their life secure will lose it, but
> those who lose their life will keep it.
> —Luke 17:33

> *But let us not forget that human knowledge and skills alone cannot
> lead humanity to a happy and dignified life.*[4]
> *—Albert Einstein (1875–1955),*
> *German-born American physicist*

33   Sabotage as hopeful?

The Luddites may have been right: channel hopefulness into destructive acts so that evil is destroyed and hope prospers. Or the Luddites may have been wrong: destroy your hopefulness and your cause by creating stronger enemies. The question for this entry: Is sabotage an act of hope or one of despair?

These weaver-populists wanted to stop an encroaching evil—the mechanization of labor—that threatened their livelihoods. They hoped by their violence to begin a revolution against the oligarchy of factory builders and owners. Their efforts failed, crushed by civil authorities when the Luddites' prophetic words were ignored by most people.

The attitudes and actions of the Luddites may pose these questions for you: "What do you do when evil quashes hope?" The Luddites had an answer: "Defeat the evil by violent means." In that sense, Luddites were terrorists and their actions a barrier to hope.

A deeper examination of their movement reveals that these folk had a positive intent: to restore an economy that would give workers hope. Luddites may have been prescient, too, because many of the world's looming environmental crises were seeded by the Industrial Revolution. Thus they could be considered savants, not just saboteurs.

The "what-to-do-about-evil" question is raised in Scripture, too: Was Jeremiah a saboteur when he subverted civil

Luddite, member of a nineteenth-century populist movement in northern England that hoped to derail the Industrial Revolution—and preserve the craft of weaving—by destroying mechanized looms

---

authority, insisting that rulers obey the "word of the LORD" he proclaimed? Was Mary advocating destruction of the powerful in her magnificent song about God's actions? Was Jesus's violent disruption of Temple commerce an act of sabotage? Were these and other biblical heroes hopeful saboteurs or did their actions just get in the way of others' hopes?

You may someday be called to answer these questions, with hopefulness as your goal and guiding principle. Perhaps the Luddites will come to mind.

Or perhaps not.

When has your subtle sabotage been helpful or hopeful?
When merely destructive?

See, I am sending you out like sheep into the midst of
wolves; so be as wise as serpents and innocent as doves.
—Matthew 10:16

All business sagacity reduces itself in the last analysis to judicious
use of sabotage.[5]
—*Thorstein Veblen (1857–1929),*
American sociologist and economist

34 Desperados unmasked

One of the legendary characters of the nineteenth-century United States' Wild West was the "desperado." Part of "the criminal element," this person was more fearful than a common outlaw. Individually or in gangs, desperados were pursued by law officers and bounty hunters, encouraged by promised rewards on WANTED posters.

What made the desperado fearsome was not just that he (or she) continued to escape punishment for dastardly acts, but that this person had become permanently dangerous to society. The desperado's criminal behavior had become a habit, a way of life fueled and founded on desperation.

Hope was not an option for desperados. A lifestyle that had started perhaps as petty crimes or one-time acts of desperation had turned into something deeper and less penetrable by hope. Desperate attitudes became desperate actions, which further strengthened the desperation. Being hunted down like animals added to the deep hopelessness desperados carried in their mental saddlebags.

If you were to find yourself deeply desperate, what might you learn from these mythical characters in this country's dusty past? You might ask yourself this question: How close are you to engaging in desperate, dangerous acts? If, in your hopelessness, you were to cross that invisible line, you could become shunned or cast off by the rest of society. You might soon slide beyond the

desperado, mock-Spanish word ("reckless criminal"), from Latin *desperare*, "without hope"

---

hope-giving reach of those around you. And once your despair had turned into habitual actions that presented danger to the general society, there would be only one direction for your life: a downward spiral.

On the other hand, it's possible that you could amend your dangerous ways and become hopeful once again. That could happen if those who loved you were also forgiving and abounding in hope.

That kind of forgiveness would itself be legendary!

Describe a real or imagined scenario in which your desperation could cross over a line.

Blessed are you when people revile you and persecute you and utter all kinds of evil against you falsely on my account. Rejoice and be glad, for your reward is great in heaven.
—Matthew 5:11–12a

Anarchy happens when desperados work together.
—*Anonymous*

Those are rare who fall without becoming degraded; there is a point, moreover, at which the unfortunate and the infamous are associated and confounded in a single word, a fatal word.[6]
—*Victor Hugo (1802–1885), French writer*

35 Forgiveness unbound

If you're not careful, your forgiveness could become insipid window dressing. Like a trophy child, wife, or husband, forgiveness might become one of those "Christian character traits" that show well publicly but don't permeate your being. In fact, trophy forgiveness might actually be a barrier to hope.

Your hope can get bogged down if, before you forgive, you always yield to the urge to find fault with, punish, or destroy the soon-to-be-forgiven one. Whose hope gets blocked? Obviously that of the person you're eventually going to forgive, but also your own. That's right—you become less hopeful if your forgiving spirit has to wait for your blaming-and-shaming spirit to do its work first.

As a accompaniment to your urge to find fault or punish, forgiveness likely excludes you from hope—revenge is a harsh master that must be satisfied first. If you tie your forgiveness to reciprocity—"I'll forgive if you confess"—then forgiveness can't bring you hope. Then forgiveness is only a transaction.

One example of forgiveness that's unbound and unbogged is restorative justice. This part of the criminal justice system helps victims of horrific crimes learn to offer forgiveness to those who committed those crimes. In turn, these despairing people often find hope even in the middle of their extended imprisonment. Where the urge to exact punishment had previously bred evil,

trophy, ultimately from Greek *tropaion,*
"a monument of an enemy's defeat"

---

now forgiveness raises its children: hopefulness, grace, and inner peace. And these offspring of forgiveness spread their influence even in prisons, places of confining despair.

Hope is a kind of reset button that restores lives. Real forgiveness—a first impulse that's freed from its restraints—is the finger that pushes that button. That's why, when unfettered by the barrier of revenge, your forgiveness can be powerful, attention attracting, and energetic.

And you won't need to show your trophies, either.

How does your forgiveness get tied up, unable to feed hope?

And forgive us our sins, for we ourselves forgive everyone
indebted to us.
—Luke 11:4a

*If thy brother wrongs thee, remember not so much his wrongdoing,
but more than ever that he is thy brother.*[7]
—Epictetus (c. 50–120),
Greek Stoic philosopher

75

36 Economy vs. ecology

Many of the barriers to your hope are likely founded on your concerns about the health of the world's economy and ecology. Although they come from the same cognate—*oikos*, household or dwelling place—economy and ecology have seemed to be at odds with each other.

The fault lies in the cognitive, not the cognative, realm. In common usage, perhaps your own, *economy* can be reduced to a singular definition, referring only to the larger system by which wealth is created and distributed. Thus your "household" would be defined only by your accumulated assets. (And if you frequently use phrases like "the bottom line" or "at the end of the day," you could be limiting "economy" to short-term ideals or outcomes.) This is a narrow way of thinking that might bog down your hopefulness because it's measured primarily by money.

Ecology might offer a more useful approach to your well-being. Here your "household" includes the entire planet and the people and creatures that live on it. If you're thinking ecologically, the sustainability of life on the earth is your primary concern. "At the end of an epoch" supplants "the end of a day."

One way to avoid getting bogged down by a narrow understanding of economy:

economy, from the Greek *oikos* (house, dwelling place, habitation) + *nomos* (managing); **ecology,** coined in the 1800s from *oikos* + *logia* (study of)

- Step 1. Think of your personal economy as part of God's larger and longer plan—*economia* can also mean the plan by which the household is managed.
- Step 2. Behave as though you are part of an ecology that sustains God's world into coming centuries.

In these ways you might be less tempted to seek only your own welfare. You could be more willing to be patient with the unfolding of your life, better able to see the big picture, more grateful for and generous with what you possess.

Maybe even more eco-cognate. . . .

How deep is your understanding of economics?

Moreover, it is required of stewards [*oikonomos*] that
they be found trustworthy.
—1 Corinthians 4:2

Socialism failed because it couldn't tell the economic truth; capitalism may
fail because it couldn't tell the ecological truth.[8]
—*Lester R. Brown (b. 1934), environmentalist, futurist*

Part 4

Skills

37 Touch, don't only look

You've come to the heart of this field guide, a place where you learn some of the requisite skills for finding hope in the fields where you live and work. Because any hope-seeking begins with heightened attention—the "looking" part of the title above— these entries will help you know how and where to focus your gaze. Because hope is as tangible as love or kindness, this section also helps you with "touching," getting close enough to hopefulness to experience it with all of your senses.

The entries in this section presume that you are honest about wanting to find hope in these times, that you have a knack for thinking beyond "thinking outside the box," that you like to explore with your eyes, your curiosity, your intelligence, your heart. That you want to help bring about God's will for the world.

You'll find these entries a valuable addition to your present skills, a complement for your present aptitudes for hope, and a mind-stretching exercise for your deepest instincts. In some entries you will be comforted, in others challenged, and in still others surprised by the thoughts you encounter. All of the entries will help you make hopefulness your preferred approach to life.

Because the emphases in these entries will move between looking and touching, you might want to mark up this part of the field guide even more than the other sections. You could assess

skill, from the Old Norse *skil,* "distinction, discernment"

---

your competency in each skill, add your own descriptions of the capabilities you read about, or recall stories about times when you've practiced these skills.

May you find joy in what you read, what you see, and what you touch.

How strong are your capacities for finding hope?

Always be ready to make your defense to anyone who
demands from you an accounting for the hope that is in you.
—1 Peter 3:15b

*It's not until you get your hands into it that
you realize dirt is actually soil.*[1]
—Tony Tyznik, landscape architect

38   Changing your thinking

When you want to change, you have two choices: think your way into acting or act your way into thinking. Let's look here at the first choice, changing your patterns of thinking. (Thinking includes the ways your brain processes sensory inputs, how it organizes itself, and the processes by which you remain self-aware.)

To strengthen hopeful thinking, you might consider any of these possibilities:

- Be honest about your basic temperament. With all your layers peeled back, who are you, really?
- Revisit situations in which you could have chosen hope but didn't. Recall the first set of thoughts that came to mind.
- Recollect your thinking at especially hopeful moments in your life. What were you thinking, and why?
- At the end of each day, give yourself a score on a "hope index" you invent.

After a week, analyze the scores for patterns that you want to strengthen or change:

- Ask people who know you what they see in your eyes in a variety of circumstances. (The concept: your eyes are the light of your soul.)
- Imagine yourself as predominantly hopeful.

index, from Latin *indicis,* "forefinger, sign, list, or anything that points out"

- If your basic spirit tends towards discouragement or frustration, ask yourself what it would take—what circumstances, influences, miracles, or experiences—for you to forsake those ways of thinking, perhaps only one step or thought at a time.
- Ask someone who loves you to remind you to resolve to keep hope as your ideal choice for approaching life.

All of these changes in thinking presume an affirmative answer to this question: "How willing are you to change your thought patterns toward basic hopefulness?" With such an answer, you will have already begun to increase hopefulness.

Or you could turn the page and try acting your way into thinking.

How else might you be mindful about your hopefulness?

> O Lord, you have searched me and known me.
> You know when I sit down and when I rise up;
> you discern my thoughts from far away.
> —Psalm 139:1–2

Despair is the hopelessness of not even being able to die.[2]
—Søren Kierkegaard

39   Changing your behaviors

Another way to become more hopeful is to change the way you act, knowing that your attitudes will likely follow. To increase your ability to change behaviors, try any of the following:

- Imitate people whose hopeful behaviors you admire. (You learn much of what you do or think from others' actions.)
- Notice the people who are mimicking your behaviors! (What good example of hopefulness do they see in you?)
- Pick one of the places where you spend significant time. Write down which of your actions in that situation might be changed to become more hopeful.
- Listen to the words you use, or reread what you write. Talk with a friend about words that get in the way of hopefulness, and words that act like sparks of hope.
- Give names to your hope-actions. (For example, Changing Gossip into Appreciation or Seeing the Big Picture.) Use the names frequently in your conversations.
- For at least one day, act as if your problems were actually opportunities. A good way to start: In difficult situations, ask yourself, "What's useful here?"
- During your end-of-day prayer time, review significant decisions you've made that day. Give each one a "hope index" score. Look for patterns you can change or strengthen, or change the content of your prayers.

change, from Latin *cambire*, "to exchange or barter"

- Recount your assets—the gifts from God that are useful. How could you put those assets together so that you could accomplish one hopeful deed?
- Make and keep one promise to yourself, regardless of its size or importance. Tomorrow add and keep another promise. (Part of being hopeful is keeping promises.)

Your hopeful actions can create hopeful thoughts, starting you on your way to even more changes.

Talk about a time when your changed actions eventually resulted in a different way of thinking.

Examine yourselves to see whether you are living
in the faith. Test yourselves. Do you not realize that
Jesus Christ is in you?
—2 Corinthians 13:5a

There should be less talk; a preaching point is not a meeting point.
What do you do then? Take a broom and clean someone's house.
That says enough.[3]
—*Mother Teresa (Agnes Gonxha Bojaxhiu) (1910–1997),*
Albanian-born nun who worked in India; beatified 2004; revered
by many as a modern saint

40 Starting with rescue

As you strengthen your hopefulness skills, you might want to start by admitting that you need to be rescued from the slime of despair. That first step can be followed immediately by the second: admitting that God is the rescuer to trust.

It isn't easy to recognize your need for rescue. On one hand, you may think that you can earn, learn, work, weasel, or will yourself into a preferred future and that you do not need God's saving hand. As long as the source for your hope is always you, you're probably not as hopeful as you are resourceful.

On the other hand, you may be just waiting around for God's miraculous salvaging of your miserable existence. In that case, you're probably not experiencing hope, either. If your hope doesn't motivate action, it may be just another variety of despairing helplessness.

Both views of hope have been overemphasized by various strands of Christian theology. Some Christians have mistaken hope for a pie-in-the-sky attitude that becomes their excuse for inaction. ("God is going to rescue us all eventually.") Others think that hope demands that they engage in frequent or fervent acts of devotion or discipleship. (Thus "you didn't pray hard enough" is supposed to encourage you to be hopeful.)

Acknowledging that you can't save yourself from despair could be a good starter skill in finding hope. Knowing that you

rescue, from Latin *excutere,* "to shake off, drive away"

---

have been, are now, and will continue to be rescued only by God—through the actions of other people—you can live past the limits of trying to be your own savior. You can avoid confusing hope with ingenuity or trust in God-as-Loving-Magician.

Faith in God's loving hand can also help create generosity—God's Spirit inspires you to bring hopeful thoughts and actions to others. Perhaps the real mark of your rescue is that you become a hope-bringing rescuer yourself.

And what a skill that would be!

> **What would it take for you to admit that
> you can't always make yourself hopeful?**

> Restore to me the joy of your salvation,
> and sustain in me a willing [generous] spirit.
> —Psalm 51:12

> *You must learn to be still in the midst of activity and to be vibrantly
> alive in repose.*[4]
> *—Indira Gandhi (1917–1984),
> prime minister of India, 1966–77, 1980–84*

41   Where does hope hide?

Like any living thing, hope has a preferred habitat, the place
where it lives best, prospering and replicating itself easily. Hope
exists in other places, though, small nooks and crannies of life that
aren't as easily identified. In these places hope incubates, grows,
and prospers out of sight, perhaps for its own protection. Some of
those hope-homes may be the fields in which you use this guide.

To find hope in its hiding places, you may need to start
looking in a different way:

- Ask more "why" questions of hopeful people.
- Get ready to find hope in unusual or difficult circumstances.
- Learn to be a quiet observer of quieting hope.
- Be fully present in situations that seem chaotic or unfamiliar.
- Look for hope in plain sight.
- Frequent "nonreligious" situations to find hope in different
  work clothes.
- Remember that hope might wait for all other attitudes to
  show themselves first.
- Spend time with people whose hopeful actions match their
  hopeful words.
- Learn the language that hopeful people use in difficult times.
- Recall past hopes that were realized over time.
- Ignore anything that distracts you from finding hope.

incubate, from Latin *incubare,* "to hatch"

- Look inside despair, anger, fear, and evil to find the spores of hope.
- Suspend your usual ways of thinking about "the bottom line" or "at the end of the day."

If you want to find the places where hope might be sequestered, waiting to be useful, you must value hope highly enough to do the necessary work of discovering its whereabouts.

Be certain of one thing: hope thrives wherever it hides.

If we can encourage and embolden, why can't we "enhope" or "emhope"?

The LORD was not in the wind. . . the LORD was not in the earthquake. . . the LORD was not in the fire; and after the fire a sound of sheer silence. When Elijah heard it, he wrapped his face in his mantle and went out and stood at the entrance of the cave.

—1 Kings 19:11–13

A growing seed can dislodge slabs of concrete.
—Anonymous

42   Where does hope hide (again)?

Whether hope was hiding or not, you've probably found hope in moments like these:

- You were at a noisy, boisterous party when you noticed another quiet person across the room, someone who seemed interesting and thoughtful.
- You were fascinated and encouraged by the stories of elderly people who lived well during the first Great Depression.
- When it seemed too late, other possibilities suddenly arose, because you thought of the situation in another way.
- After a difficult divorce (or a financial downturn, complete rejection, or job loss), your life was redeemed by the undeserved grace, forgiveness, or love of another person.
- In the presence of a hopeful person, you suddenly realized how much that person was like you.
- You watched a cynical or desperate person completely disarmed by thoughtful, calming conversation.
- Someone you admired helped you realize your abundant assets in a difficult time.
- A person who is poor told you how she or he was "blessed by God."
- Someone completely buried in hopelessness strengthened your resolve to avoid that attitude and its resulting outcomes.

wonder, from Old English *wunder,* "marvel, marvelous thing, the object of astonishment"

In each of these experiences, you were likely discovering hope peeking out from its hiding place and encouraging you to look more carefully. Now, as you grow in your observing skills, you may realize that hope is not hiding, after all. Now that you know where and how to look, hope is apparent in all aspects of life, ready for your appreciation and gratitude. With better vision, you will probably start to see hope everywhere.

And won't that be wonderful!

How else might you learn to see hope in its hiding places?

Iron sharpens iron,
and one person sharpens the wits of another.
—Proverbs 27:17

Hope hides inside hopeful people, some of whom know you well.
—Anonymous

43   Spotting the hopeful ones

You can find hopeful people by looking at their faces, words, actions, and relationships. Here's why:
- People's faces reflect the hope inside their brains.
- Their words show hopeful attitudes.
- Their actions reveal a hopeful stance.
- Hopeful people congregate.

Here's what else you can look for: Because they're pragmatists, they're not satisfied that either pessimism or optimism works all that well. For hopeful folk the glass is neither half-empty (pessimistic) nor half-full (optimistic) but always completely full (practical). That makes them shrewd in the face of seeming impossibilities. (Remember the ground controllers' request to the astronauts in the disabled Apollo 13 capsule: "Tell us what you have up there.")

The hopeful ones are certainly not Pollyannas. (This popular early-twentieth-century fictional heroine invented "The Glad Game," which spawned generations of positive thinkers and supplied the gooey pejorative cast to her name.) Because they're painfully aware of problems and persistent about solving unpleasant difficulties, hopeful folk are not always cheerful or pleasant. (Think about the farmers you know!)

dour, from Latin *durus*, "hard"

You can spot hopeful people because they're thoughtful, aware, focused, realistic, purposeful, active, relational, and powerful. Their wrinkle lines aren't dour furrows. In conversation, hopeful people don't go along with bashing, moaning, whining, or criticizing. They are generous in interpreting others' motives. They understand the "thou shalt" parts of the Ten Commandments as well as the "thou shalt not" portions. They have calluses on their hands.

If that's who they are and how you find them, just where are these "hopeful ones"?

You can find them almost anywhere your eyes go.

> **Why do you think hopeful people congregate?**
> **How about despairing people?**

> Just as water reflects the face,
> so one human heart reflects another.
> —Proverbs 27:19

Instead of always harping on a man's faults, tell him of his virtues. Try to pull him out of his rut of bad habits. Hold up to him his better self, his REAL self that can dare and do and win out! [5]
—*Pollyanna Whittier, in Eleanor H. Porter's book* Pollyanna

44   Profile: Hanging around Anika

You'd love being with Anika, spending some downtime with her. A capable parent, spouse, and employee, Anika is working to eliminate world hunger through her family life and her profession. Intelligent and generous, she's one of the hopeful ones whose lifework leapfrogs frustration to span the world. Knowing Anika might help you repair the places where your hopeful identity or behaviors have become shabby, weak, or empty.

Anika has been really good at ferreting out hope wherever she finds herself—even during the year when several of her close friends died suddenly. You could discover her emotional stability and understand that she sees worth in almost every situation, every person.

Because she knows that she's only partially in control of circumstances—she works inside a large bureaucracy—Anika could help you realize how to be flexible. Because she fights the evils of hunger and poverty, Anika could teach you how to direct your anger toward changing the future to positive outcomes. In her listening presence, you could become more patient, more positive, more accepting of others. She could be your example for thinking before talking.

Because she knows stories of how hope happens all around the world, Anika could help you trust the capacities of any group of people to organize themselves in active solutions to their problems.

solidarity, from French *solidaire,* "interdependent, complete, entire"

Anika is clever and resourceful, so she could show you how to seek and find water where others see only drought. She could introduce you to the people and places that help her find inspiration, meaning, and imagination. She could tell you about her wider worlds, how they include pleasure, community, and solidarity.

Soaking up hope in the presence of Anika—or of any other hopeful ones you know who match her description—would take more than one conversation. More than one story.

So bring your appointment calendar.

What would it take for you to spend quality time with someone hopeful?

[Martha] had a sister named Mary, who sat at the Lord's feet and listened to what he was saying. But Martha was distracted by her many tasks.
—Luke 10:39–40a

All those who try to go it sole alone,
Too proud to be beholden for relief,
Are absolutely sure to come to grief.[6]
—Robert Frost

45 Hope lives in conversation

Conversation is more than talking. A better synonym for this important human activity might be *accompaniment* or *presence*. So you never "just talk." (Oĸ, maybe you "just talk" when you text, chat, chirp, or twitter.) In true conversations, you spend quality time with another person. The words you use? They're trail markers that recall the experiences you share, the deep relationships you keep, the intimate emotions and thoughts that blossom.

Think, for example, how love can begin with a long, lingering conversation—perhaps deep into the night—when two people discover their similarities. That one conversation can become the first of many tendrils that eventually become a living bond of friendship and more.

What makes conversations into effective occasions to learn or strengthen hope? Conversational skills themselves—listening and being appreciative, honest, positive, and personal—are certainly required ingredients. More important, though, conversations meld you into relationships with other people—good places to find hope. Conversations require you to slow down your thinking and acting—giving hope a chance to find a place in the pace of the rest of your life. Stress is reduced in your conversations—especially if talk is accompanied by touch. Once again, hope can find an opening for reorganizing your brain.

conversation, from the Latin *conversari,* "to live with, keep company with, have dealings with others"

When you're conversing about important matters, you're able to persuade and be persuaded, to imagine, to mimic others' feelings, and to draw courage from their example—all seedbeds for hope. Once planted, conversations keep your hope well nourished.

One more gift that conversations offer: the strong possibility that those moments of intimate sharing won't fade from your memory, that they'll engender other moments, that you'll carve out future opportunities to share hope with your conversational partners.

Makes you want to do more than "just talk" with someone, doesn't it?

Review in your mind the hope you found in a recent conversation.

And [Joseph] kissed all his brothers and wept upon them;
and after that his brothers talked with him.
—Genesis 45:15

Eighty percent of life is showing up.[7]
—*Woody Allen (b. 1935), writer, actor, director*

46 Hopeful words

You're sold on hope, and you're ready to have a meaningful conversation. But what about finding the words you'll need to communicate hope? How do you accumulate and use a "hope vocabulary"? Good questions that deserve good answers.

The first step is to pull word-weeds—any vocabulary that chokes out hope—from your normal patterns of communication. Limit the times when you grouse instead of rejoice, blame instead of confess, frown instead of chortle, criticize instead of appreciate, or talk disparagingly about someone instead of telling about their valued traits. Eliminate language that's devoid of positive emotions or festooned with the negative yammerings of some current churchly speech. Above all, discard from your daily vocabulary any words that chew up, put down, or zero-out others.

Once you've removed the problem words, think how you might have fun with words that sparkle, ennoble, grace, forgive, inspire, cut to the core, create positive feelings, or show appreciation or gratitude.

Now think how you might substitute hopeful expressions for despair- or fear-infested speech. What might happen if you played around with the prepositions you attach to hope? (See Entry 47, "Playing with prepositions," for more about this subject.) What if you enlivened your list of nouns and verbs for *hope* and *hoping*? (See the following entry, "Free hope vocabulary.")

communicate, from Latin *communicare;*
literal root "to make common"

Where can you find hope words? They're likely waiting for you in Gospel-based sermons, prayers that do more than beg for God's problem solving, letters of thanks in your congregational newsletter, training materials for church-based community organizing. Perhaps also in surprising cards, letters, phone calls, e-mails, and text messages. (Yes, maybe even in tweets!) When you find those words, put them into a list you can use the next time you want to express yourself hopefully.

And then you'll be ready to be a hope-filled communicator!

> **What hope-ruining words and expressions are
> you willing to discard for good?**

> And the Word became flesh and lived among us.
> —John 1:14a

> *I used to think I was poor. Then they told me I wasn't poor, I was
> needy. They told me it was self-defeating to think of myself as needy,
> I was deprived. Then they told me underprivileged was overused.
> I was disadvantaged. I still don't have a dime. But I have a great
> vocabulary.*[8]
> —*Jules Feiffer (b. 1929), cartoonist and writer*

Bonus! Free hope vocabulary

This bonus entry presents you with a handy-dandy vocabulary that you can draw on anytime you want to express—or find—hopefulness in yourself. Apply the list as soon as possible, because the words will take up residence in your brain as soon as you use them!

Hope verbs

Trust, anticipate, await, aspire, contemplate, count on, rely, look forward, expect, believe.

Hope nouns

Confidence, reliance, trust, faith, expectation, desire, prospect, expectancy, assumption, ambition, buoyancy.

Hope noun antonyms

Despair, surrender, fear, doubt, hopelessness, despondency, pessimism, foreboding, melancholy, futility, finality, incorrigibility.

Hopeful adjectives

Promising, encouraging, favorable, auspicious, heartening, cheering, cheerful, reassuring, optimistic, confident, sanguine, rosy, bright, plucky.

vocabulary, from Latin *vocabulum,* "word, name, noun,"
from *vocare* "to name, call"

Hopeful adjective antonyms

Dejected, hopeless, pessimistic, despondent, dim, cloudy, unfavorable, glum, abject, disconsolate, incurable, useless, impossible, ill-omened, ominous, irrevocable, pointless, defeatist.

See any words you like? See any you'd like to take out with the trash?

Just for fun

Use as many *hope* and *hopeful* words as you can to describe a person who has taught you to be more hopeful. How do the words add to your appreciation of this person?

Just for work

On a small card, write all the antonyms for hope and hopeful that you want to get rid of. Keep the card with you, and at the end of one week see how well you've done.

Just for curiosity

Write a thank-you letter to someone who's down right now. Use as many of the hope and hopeful words as possible.

Just for prayer

Imagine getting a letter filled with hopeful words. How would that feel? How long would the feeling last?

47 Playing with prepositions

Wordsmiths never meet a preposition with which they can't end a sentence. These denizens of Dictionary Land change prepositions in sentences to see what happens to the words around. (These syntactical semigeeks also know that to do its work, the preposition ending the previous sentence requires an object, as in "around these delightful little pieces of grammar and syntax.")

What does this have to do with hope? A simple answer: by exploring how prepositions affect your use of hope-words, you expand your capacity to think about hope as well as to foster hope among other people. (For example, what would happen if you talked about "hope alongside" as well as "hope in"?)

Another reason to broaden your use of prepositions with hope-words: hope can move beyond nice idea into something more powerful and inclusive. (Try "hope over _____" for a while.) If your hope-language is limited in any way, it's possible that your understanding, practice, and proclamation of hope are also limited. Your patterns of hope-speech can become hackneyed, trite, or boring.

Think what might happen to a hope-sentence when you change its prepositions. For example, what's the difference between "hope for people who are poor" and "hope in people who are poor"? What would any hope-utterance proclaim if you insisted on the grand preposition *throughout* every time you

preposition, ultimately from Latin *præponere,* "put before"

---

described hope? Think how hope would always connect you to others if *among* accompanied your use of *hope.* (Or see hope's meanings expand as you substitute various prepositions in the sample sentence below in this entry's margin.)

As you continue to improve your skills as a hoping person, take time to play with prepositions. Doing so may help you understand how wordsmiths think about, with, around, inside, and outside words.

Your playing might also help your hoping.

Possible prepositions

at, from, in, inside, outside, of, for, with, to, over, under, around, on, through, among, by, beside, throughout, within

Sample sentence

Hope [insert preposition] God is a wondrous thing to behold.

Forgive, and you will be forgiven; give, and it will be given to you. A good measure, pressed down, shaken together, running over, will be put into your lap; for the measure you give will be the measure you get back.
—Luke 6:37–38

48   What's a prophet to do now?

You have enough hope, you have words, and you want to say something about hope. You're ready to be a hope-prophet, a "forth-teller" who talks and writes about hope. What skills do you need?

Certainly you're going to need to polish up your proficiencies to warn about dangers and punishments. You'll probably want to refine your abilities to fume, accuse, name names, make trouble, and face down enemies. Great work if you can get it!

Another set of hope-prophet skills, though, might be more necessary for these times. As a hope-prophet, you can invite, cajole, persuade, comfort, and delight people. Some of your work might involve translating; the writers of Scripture spoke to their situations, but their words need transposing into today's realities.

To get ready to be a prophet, you'll need to spend time rereading the Old and New Testament poets and prophets—yes, Jesus was one of them. You'll scour news stories and the writings of social critics for their prophetic wisdom. You'll probably have to dig back into the New Testament letters, where hope pops up like a spring flower. You'll read, listen, and listen some more—all in an attempt to discern what's really happening inside and around people. You'll pray.

invite, from Latin *invitare,* "to invite, treat, entertain;" originally likely "to be pleasant toward"

And when you're ready, you'll strap on your people skills, your words—see previous entries here—and your sense of calling to foster hope. You'll go where you have always gone, among people who already know you, but with a different way of thinking and speaking. By your words, you will speak of how hope can change people's lives—even in these times. By your actions, you will gentle people away from fearful individualism. By your prayers, you will strengthen resolve and bring energy to lives straining toward hope.

Yes, you will be a prophet.

When and where do you feel pulled toward a prophetic role in your lifework?

Would that all the LORD people were prophets, and that the LORD would put his spirit on them!
—Numbers 11:29a

The easiest kind of relationship is with ten thousand people; the hardest is with one.
—widely attributed to Joan Baez (b. 1941), singer, activist

49   Looking out the windows

It may be obvious, but to be skilled at hope, you have to look around. What may not be obvious is that you have to open up and look out the windows of your life. These are all the places where you can peer past what's normal, confining, or expected. God places hope in every corner of the world, within every human brain. So why would you want to limit your understanding or appreciation of hope to your own circumstances? (And by the way, mirrors aren't windows; you don't learn a lot about the world God loves by looking only at yourself.)

To be skilled at hoping, you need to accept the Spirit's invitation to look—and listen—past your usual surroundings. Your windows? They might include blogs and social interaction sites, weekly coffee klatches, fiction and nonfiction books, Bible study groups, purposed travel, movies, or e-mails from your adult children. Your view might include the physical and social sciences, the arts, theology, business and industry, diplomacy, government, politics, and the daily news. Future studies, women's studies, and cultural studies might invite you to gaze at their special landscapes.

When you look out those windowpanes, God also invites you to come out from the confines of your usual definitions or practices of hope. God can bless a different frame of reference and help you understand hope from inside the viewpoints of others.

window, from Old Norse *vindauga,* literally "wind eye"

You can't travel the entire world, know every culture, or meet every hopeful person, but you can come to one new window and look out. You can read in one new field, start one new conversation, or dig more deeply into one already familiar scripture. You can reexamine your family history to see how you have inherited hope.

Whatever the new windows, enjoy your view of hope!

What new windows have you opened in your life?

By faith we understand that the worlds were prepared by the word of God, so that what is seen was made from things that are not visible.
—Hebrews 11:3

Hope begins in the dark, the stubborn hope that if you just show up and try to do the right thing, the dawn will come. You wait and watch and work: You don't give up.[9]
—Anne Lamott (1954), novelist, nonfiction writer, and determined Christian

50 Small trends, tiny data

One of the most important hope-finding or hope-strengthening skills you can acquire is the ability to see in small things what others may have overlooked. Even if you have some ambivalence about looking for hope in statistics—"Lies, damned lies, and statistics" may come to mind—it's assuring to find in trends or facts some evidence that hope is alive and well.

Because hope can appear small, you may have to work hard at seeing evidences of hope all around you. Consultant, author, and futurist Paul Hawken (*Blessed Unrest*) says, for example, that most of us may have missed "one of the greatest movements in history," a massive effort at bringing hopeful change to literally thousands of seemingly hopeless situations around the world. His anecdotes are compelling, and his numbers may be right.

How might you increase your skill to turn over rocks, look behind curtains, or peer around corners to find indications of hope? Consider these possibilities:

- Read obituaries to find stories of world-changing lives.
- Analyze tables and charts in business news sources.
- Enter the name or title of any hope-related idea into your favorite Internet search engine.
- Keep track of trend indicators such as polls or surveys.
- Read or visit websites maintained by futurists or behavioral economists (for example, www.faithpopcorn.com).

propaganda, from Latin *propagare,* "to propagate"

- Visit government data banks (see www.data.gov or www.census.gov).

What are you looking for? Facts that go beyond propaganda or marketing slogans. Hopeful ideas that are sprouting as new businesses or organizations, the number of websites devoted to hope-related subjects, books that are selling well, social-networking sites aimed at hope, the increase in sale of hope-related products (for example, gardening products). Remember that what you find may be small now, but may grow more significant over time.

That's how it is with hope!

What small, hopeful trends are you paying attention to?

Not one of them [sparrows] will fall to the ground apart from your Father. And even the hairs on your head are all counted. So do not be afraid; you are of more value than many sparrows.
—Matthew 10:29b–30

The death of one man is a tragedy.
The death of millions is a statistic.[10]
—Erich Maria Remarque (1898–1970), German writer,
author of All Quiet on the Western Front

Profile: Critical incident management

Hope is more than an ideal for Von. Von teaches people how to hope. You might think from this description that Von's a professor of theology, a sociologist, a psychologist, a pastor, or at least a writer of books about hope.

Nope, not even close. Von teaches law-enforcement leaders how to be hopeful in critical incidents they will likely face in their profession. (A critical incident might be anything from a natural disaster to a prolonged hostage situation.) What makes the incident critical is that if it's not handled correctly, people will be injured, or worse. That's why Von characterizes the value of his training this way: "Without hope," he says, "they'd die."

During his career as a member of the armed forces, a law-enforcement officer, and a police chief, Von has learned some important principles for staying alive. In situations where survival depends on every decision, it's important that law-enforcement officers not be hypervigilant. Overawareness of details can result in an officer's being overwhelmed by a tidal wave of information. A brain filled with information—most of it fearsome—is not able to analyze, imagine possible actions and their likely outcomes, make a careful choice, prepare for action, or execute that action correctly.

In these situations, Von notes, hope is a crucial mental activity. More than mere optimism or wishful thinking, hope

critical, from Greek *kritikos,* "able to make judgments"

---

settles minds, encourages the brain to work well, and undergirds decision-making processes with confidence about positive outcomes.

A man of deep faith, Von knows the theological foundations for hope and understands that hope comes from God's gracious outpouring of gifts. But in his line of work, theoretical propositions about hopefulness take a back seat to one important fact: hope helps people survive.

Sleep peacefully tonight, knowing that people like Von are out there!

Where in your daily life does hope have a decidedly practical cast to it?

I urge you now to keep up your courage, for there will be no loss of life among you, but only of the ship.
—Paul, speaking to storm-tossed sailors in Acts 27:22

In these times, are we living in a "prolonged critical incident"?[11]
—*Von (last name withheld)*

52   Asking around

Use the following survey to assess how hopeful you might be.[12]
For fun, compare your results with those of others. For other
ideas, see the Scoring Guide below.

YES NO

❏ ❏ 1. There are times when my despair gets bigger than I
can handle.

❏ ❏ 2. I have clothing with hopeful or hope-related
messages on it.

❏ ❏ 3. I am sure that the times ahead are going to be
worse than they are now.

❏ ❏ 4. People around me tell me that I'm fairly positive
and hopeful.

❏ ❏ 5. There are times when I feel trapped by my
circumstances in life.

❏ ❏ 6. My prayers are more about gratitude than about
asking God for help.

❏ ❏ 7. Many of my conversations include blaming,
whining, or moaning.

❏ ❏ 8. I think I could be a good example for hopefulness.

❏ ❏ 9. Most leaders are clueless about really solving
society's problems.

❏ ❏ 10. My hope vocabulary is fairly well developed, and I
use it often.

assess, from Latin *assessus,* "to sit beside"

❑ ❑ 11. I'm drawn to media that describe the world's problems accurately.

❑ ❑ 12. I hear a lot of hope in sermons, prayers, and lessons at weekly worship.

❑ ❑ 13. Most trends in the world are headed irrevocably downward.

❑ ❑ 14. I don't spend much time with people who bring down my spirits.

❑ ❑ 15. Environmental and economic collapse are punishments for us all.

Scoring Guide

For every "yes" answer on odd-numbered items, give yourself 2 points. For every "yes" answer on even-numbered items, give yourself 3 points. Subtract the total of odd-numbered items from the total of even-numbered items. This is your "hope index score."

Which items took awhile to answer? Why?

Which questions do you wish you had been asked? Why?

How do you know if someone's basically hopeful?

Which of your answers surprised you? Why?

53   Living in the movement

One necessary life skill is the ability to know where you are at any moment. (A field guide can help you determine your location.) One way to situate your current place in history is to see yourself as part of a movement. That's right, a movement—an encompassing, energetic change in direction or attitude—that's moving toward hopeful outcomes. Even in the middle of these difficult times!

Movements are hard to spot. Their parts are so small that they're nearly invisible, and yet as a whole, the movement is so pervasive that you can't see it from a larger perspective, either. Unlike revolutions, wars, or epochs, movements don't have names; this also makes them difficult to pin down or describe. Even so, futurist Paul Hawken and his associates have estimated that there may be as many as two million organizations worldwide that are working toward ecological sustainability and social justice.

If you're acting hopefully, you're part of this movement! You've become part of a flotilla that defies the mantra "The ocean is so big and my boat so small." If you were to fly over this vast armada, you'd see the similarities among the ships that make up this fleet. You'd see each of the movement's organizations whittling down the size of society's problems, each band of fervent followers infecting others with their zeal and insistence. You'd soon notice the spiritual quality of many parts of the

mantra, from Sanskrit *mantra,* literally
"instrument of thought"

---

movement, many of them Christian. And if you watched carefully, you'd sense how this movement is growing at its edges, how it's slowly surrounding and enveloping those who still believe in war, who still despair about the human condition, who still see themselves as deserving of everything they can grab.

Yes, you're part of something big, something good and God-graced. That makes this a good place to find yourself.

Rejoice that you are living in this movement!

How does it feel to be part of something as big as a movement?

Therefore, since we are surrounded by so great a cloud
of witnesses, let us also lay aside every weight and the sin
that clings so closely, and let us run with perseverance the
race that is set before us, looking to Jesus the pioneer and
perfecter of our faith.
—Hebrews 12:1–2a

*History tends by its very nature to obscure the mundane acts that are the
harbingers of change.*[13]
—*Paul Hawken, in* Blessed Unrest

Part 5

Actions

54   Hope is as hope does

The collapse of the world isn't going to be stopped or slowed by well-meaning people who only know about hope or who only think hopefully. Because hope motivates people, the value of hope is in the actions it engenders. That's what this section of *It's Not Too Late* is about—thoughts about possible deeds you and others might imagine and undertake once you find hope. Because you can act your way into thinking, the actions suggested in these entries may also result in your becoming more hopeful.

You're the only person who can decide if and how you want to begin acting more hopefully. That's why the entries in this section don't presume to tell you what to do. That's why they don't attempt to wow you with tales of the creative feats you might accomplish if only you were talented beyond measure and possessed of unlimited assets. Instead, these entries serve as gentle nudges toward actions, ideas that help you approach your own tipping points—the moments in your life when you decide to take action, no matter how small.

You might want to read some of these entries more than once, photocopy them for sharing, or use them as discussion starters in a group. You might search these entries for God's answer to a question that has likely occurred to you earlier: "Dear Lord, what could I do next?"

act, from Latin *agere,* "to do, set in motion, drive, urge chase, stir up"

Before entering this section, you might take time to reflect—alone or with others—about what you've read here that has stirred anything new or familiar in your soul. You might find others with whom to have a deeper conversation about your lifework—what you want to accomplish in life. Or you might just see what you've read so far works in the worlds you inhabit every day.

God keep you active in hope!

What or who compels you to act hopefully?

May the God of hope fill you with all joy and peace in believing,
so that you may abound in hope by the power of the Holy Spirit.
—Romans 15:13

You must first walk around a bit before you can understand the
distance from the valley to the mountain.[1]
—*Bhutanese proverb*

55 Imagining something different

"What you can imagine, you can do." This maxim carries the weight of applied neuroscience, suggesting the first step you might take to move away from despair: visualizing yourself engaged in hopeful actions. Imagination in this case is not merely creative thought—brainstorming, for example—although the two ideas are probably cousins. Perhaps triggered by "mirror neurons"— brain cells that connect actions you observe with your own movement—imagined action draws together a full array of your brain's capabilities to join intent and accomplishments.

Try any of the following imagination-starters to see how your brain might approach hopeful actions:

- Picture yourself in a sunny meadow, where signposts point toward hopeful actions in a variety of directions. Each sign promises what's possible; in the distance you can see evidence that the signs are telling the truth. Decide which direction you will take.

- Suppose that you are trapped in a difficult situation. Suddenly someone else shows up, unfazed by the problem. He or she points out a solution that you missed and offers you the time and energy to explore that possibility. Who is that person and what will you do?

- In your mind visualize a billboard that features an overwhelming environmental or economic problem. Now

imagine, from the Latin *imaginere,* "to form an image of, represent," ultimately from imago, "copy, statue, picture, idea, appearance."

---

imagine yourself climbing around to the other side of the billboard. You find written there in small letters another aspect of this situation, one that's hopeful. Now write on the front of the billboard how you will respond to this hopeful descriptor. Do what you wrote.

As you imagine, remember that you are not godlike—some things are indeed not possible for you. At the same time, don't limit your imagination to what's in front of you. Let your senses and your spirit soar, and see what happens.

May the Holy Spirit be with you!

What's the best place and time for you to be imaginative?
How do you know?

Then God said, "Let us make humankind in our image,
according to our likeness."
—Genesis 1:26a

*You can't do something hopeful if you use the same kind of
thinking that created your despair in the first place.*
—Adapted from self-help axiom

56　No inconsequential acts

One of the truisms of complexity theory is that everything is connected. (Naturalist John Muir used the word *hitched* to describe this reality.) A corollary: everything causes—and is caused by—everything else, however invisibly or unpredictably. (The classic relationship between the flap of a butterfly's wings and the formation of typhoons in Asia is the most-often-cited example.) In his *Blessed Unrest*, futurist Paul Hawken recounts scores of anecdotes about the far-reaching results of seemingly small, hope-filled actions. He shows how one group multiples itself, how one small accomplishment leverages larger results, and how one idea sparks accumulated potential.

What's operating here? The power of suggestion, hard-wired skills of observation and mimicry, the nearly instantaneous spread of emotion among humans, the self-organizing potential of social groups.

It stands to reason, then, that small steps are indeed the core actions from which hopeful change is created. (Think "viral change.") What's small becomes what's big; what's ordinary becomes what's extraordinary; what's invisible becomes what's hard to ignore. That's why your smallest hopeful actions are part of a large movement—spread over time and space—that is ultimately powerful, perhaps overwhelmingly.

hitched, from Middle English *icchen,* "to move with a jerk, stir," probably referring to "hitching up pants or boots with a jerk"

A side note about not acting: your inaction—one of your brain's responses to fearsome situations—has large consequences. If you don't act in any way, you eventually lose the capacity to act. Your inaction gives more muscle to the actions of others. Because your personal resources are not directed at a hopeful result, your personal power is hidden or padlocked.

As you move toward hopeful actions, you can draw strength from the truth that there are no idle conversations, no inconsequential acts, no useless assets, no "little people." You can start taking small steps everywhere they are possible.

And you may even stop filling your self-concept and your prayers with "just" or "only."

When has one of your smallest hopeful acts resulted in something larger than you first imagined?

A little yeast leavens the whole batch of dough.
—Galatians 5:9

There are no inconsequential acts,
only consequential inaction.[2]
—Paul Hawken (b. 1946),
American futurist, environmentalist

57 What are you thinking?

No, really, what are you thinking? It's a simple question, and worth asking repeatedly, if only to keep burrowing under automatic or habitual thoughts to prepare for deeper, sustainable actions that could foster hope in your life. Being mindful of your emotional and rational thoughts can help you stay hopeful when it feels easier not to think at all.

Answer these hope-related questions about the ways you think. See what you can learn about your tendencies and temptations regarding hope.

- What parts of your thought-life feel dull, limp, routine, or emptied of hope?
- Where and when do your most hopeful thoughts hold sway?
- What kinds of thoughts keep you from even considering hope?
- What kinds of thought patterns do you use to move "hope" from good idea to action?
- What actions do you take to jump-start hopeful thoughts?
- When was the last time you felt energized to take on a seemingly intractable problem?
- When do you notice that you're just fooling yourself about your hopefulness?
- What kinds of thoughts help you sort through your confusion about economic or environmental problems?

ruminate, from Latin *ruminare,* "to chew the cud, turn over in one's mind"

- When do you take a sabbath rest away from despair or desperation?
- How do you take stock of your general emotional makeup?
- How do you know you're a hopeful person?

To remain an active hoper, you might need to try techniques that help you identify, focus on, and cherish the ways in which you think hopefully. Or you might rewrite any of the questions in this entry—substitute the word *despair* for *hope*—to discover the places where despair might have shoved aside hope and become your default frame of mind. As you ruminate, thank God for your capabilities to really think.

It's a gift, after all.

> When was the last time you spent some quality time examining your ways of thinking? What did you learn?

> I say to everyone among you not to think of yourself more highly than you ought to think, but to think with sober judgment, each according to the measure of faith that God has assigned.
> —Romans 12:3

The habit of thinking is the habit of gaining strength.[3]
—Nigerian proverb

58 Start here

Here are some potential places to begin—or restart—your hopeful journey through life. Think of each action as a kind of START HERE square on the game board of your life.

- Thank personally anyone whom you notice engaged in a hopeful act.
- Start an online or offline correspondence with someone with whom you could trade hopeful encouragements.
- Plant something, anything. (When asked what he would do if he knew that Judgment Day was coming tomorrow, Martin Luther said, "Plant an apple tree.")
- Engage in a small, hopeful act over and over again, until someone else joins you or mimics your actions.
- Buy something hopeful—a candle or a flower—and then give it away.
- In a letter, e-mail, or phone message, thank a public official or leader for a hopeful action that he or she has taken.
- Patronize neighborhood stores that need your business.
- Talk with people who provide you service—repairmen, ushers, wait staff—about the importance of their work for the rest of society.
- "Adopt" a high-school or college student in your congregation.

game, from Old English *gamen,* "joy, fun, amusement"
within the context of "people together"

- Invent a new kind of mission trip that avoids "poverty tourism" or other varieties of "ain't it awful" thinking.
- Form a small group that helps congregation members write family histories.
- Invest attention, time, or money in a green company.

As you take any of these steps, be ready for what might come next. Why? Hopeful actions beget hopeful thinking, which becomes the start for more hopeful actions.

This might be how you can keep your hope-life active and moving along.

What starting places for hope have you experienced in life?

Whoever says, "I abide in him," ought to walk just as he walked.
—1 John 2:6

Even the longest journey must begin where you stand.[4]
—*Chinese proverb*

59   Attention deficits

If you want to begin acting hopefully, first you have to pay attention. Attention is the grandmother of action. Attention connects you to your emotions, the starting places for your decisions. Once you've decided, then you take action.

Along the way from attention to action, though, you might encounter some attention deficits. In the case of hope, they're similar to the difficulties some students face when parts of their brains don't allow them to take advantage of learning activities. To engage yourself or others in hopeful actions, you need to avoid or correct attention-deficit problems such as these:

- Overattention to danger, which inhibits or prohibits anyone's ability to learn hope
- Attention that's divided among too many hopeful possibilities, which can diminish the quantity or quality of the hope that you apply to a specific situation
- Others' inattention to your pronouncements or invitations—perhaps because you don't deserve their attention!
- Your lack of concentration on preferred next steps, once you've garnered someone's attention or focused your own attention

On a more hopeful note, you're most likely a leader now because others are paying attention to you. They've seen you as

attention, from Latin *intendere,* literally "to stretch toward"

---

someone to whom attention must be paid. You're a person whose hopeful thoughts and actions benefit them. You're able to focus on their emotions, ideals, thoughts, or questions without exhibiting hurried distractedness.

Most likely you have already given these people your own appreciative attention. You've let them know you have noticed them, that you are interested in their lives, and that their potential as hopeful people is important to you.

Your most hope-filled actions, then, might be to pay attention to others, to steward carefully the limited attention you get, and to think of others' attention as a precious gift.

Grandma would like this.

Why do you think people pay attention to you?

I have called you by name, you are mine.
—Isaiah 43:1b

When you do the common things in life in an uncommon way, you will command the attention of the world.[5]
—*George Washington Carver (ca. 1861–1943),*
American botanist

60 Parenting hopefully

As the future lurches toward you, you may be wondering about the generations that will follow you. If you're a parent, the matter might be more urgent and perhaps more difficult to think about. You may be alarmed at the prospect that your children will live in a world drastically different from the one you inherited. You may be feeling guilty about your own excess, your own ignorance, your own avoidance of what surely is coming.

None of those responses may be helpful. What might be better is to think with others about how you might be a hopeful parent, even while you admit that economic and environmental collapse will color every facet of your children's lives.

To be a hopeful parent in these times, you might

- increase the number of emotionally honest conversations you have with your children about their future world;

- review and write your family history, noting the times when your ancestors overcame adversity;

- start thinking about a new framework for your parenting— one aimed especially at the skills and attitudes by which your children might prosper and remain faithful in a world of diminished resources and diminished outcomes;

- delete from your vocabulary and yearnings the notion that "being happy" is your goal for your children;

parent, from Latin *parentem,* "mother, father, ancestor," ultimately from *parere,* "to bring forth, give birth to, produce"

- think and pray about how your children will be able to change the world, whether as leaders or followers;
- do hopeful things together as a family. Think of generosity, gratitude, and graciousness as guidelines for those experiences. Use ideas from this field guide;
- stop pursuing empty goals for your life together. Start now.

However you work at this, hope can be a action guide for your parenting and a standard by which you measure your effectiveness.

May God bless your efforts.

How might an emotionally honest conversation with your children feel?

Train children in the right way;
and when old, they will not stray.
—Proverbs 22:6

You didn't have a choice about the parents you inherited, but you do have a choice about the kind of parent you will be.[6]
—Marian Wright Edelman (b. 1939),
founder and president, Children's Defense Fund

61   Kids will be kids

The future belongs to children. That's why the most hopeful action you might take is to help children and teenagers gain the skills and attitudes they will need for their futures. Considering the environmental and economic circumstances they will face in the near and long term, we're not talking about just piano lessons, soccer skills, or computer acumen.

Much of what they will face may be as yet unknown to them, or to you. If the predictions are accurate, today's children and teens will need new kinds of basic life skills, as well as the ability to find satisfaction and meaning, regardless of the shape of their lifestyles. Those capabilities might include these:

- The ability to live life at a slower pace, with fewer possessions
- Self-differentiation, which can serve as a kind of barrier to peer pressures and the fads they produce
- Self-reliance, a kind of shrewd creativity that is based on children's and teens' knowledge of their assets.
- Flexibility and nimbleness to survive in almost every circumstance
- The ability to find pleasure in what others might ignore or find ordinary
- Social intelligence, a set of characteristics that help children and teens prosper within the groups of which they are a part

vulnerable, from Latin *vulnerare,* "to wound."

- Spiritual disciplines such as prayer, confession, forgiveness, or devotion to God's will
- The skills to critique contemporary culture in a useful way
- Awareness of the world around them and the world within them

The children and teens you love are going to face a world in which they will be especially vulnerable—not only physically but also emotionally and spiritually. Preparing them for their future is a sacred privilege you have as parent or caregiver.

No doubt about it: the results of your work will build the future.

How can you be a hope-trainer for children and teens you know?

[We know that] suffering produces endurance, and endurance produces character, and character produces hope, and hope does not disappoint us.
—Romans 5:3–5a

One never goes so far as when one doesn't know where one is going.[7]
—Johann Wolfgang von Goethe (1749–1832),
German poet and dramatist

62 You're hopeful when ...

Sometimes you just need to know whether hopeful applies to you. Here's a semi-whimsical list of characteristics and actions you can use to see if the adjective applies to you and your actions.

You're hopeful when ...

- You don't mind being "the only one who thinks like that."
- You turn more than one OFF switch in your life to ON.
- You usually know what to do in tough times.
- You're already finding a way out of difficulties before others have realized that there's a problem.
- Folks around you keep asking your thoughts on important matters.
- Almost everything around you and in you is useful for something.
- You don't sweat the small stuff because you believe most stuff is small.
- You take risks on behalf of others.
- Your prayers of thanks outrace your prayers of need.
- You do good things because you want to, not because you have to.
- You are willing to wait.
- You don't attend "pity parties," even when friends invite you to that kind of conversation.

perky, from Old French *perquer,* "to perch;"
earliest meanings refer to actions of birds

- People don't normally use the terms *bright-eyed, cute, nice, spry,* or *perky* to describe you.
- You gave up on fighting, fleeing, and freezing because you found out they didn't work.

OK, OK, this checklist isn't a scientific instrument. But it raises an important question: When do you know whether you're a hopeful person? What are your action indicators of hope-filled people? How can you spot one of them on the street, around their friends, in a meeting? Who gets to decide who's hopeful and who's despairing? And what might happen if none of the items on this list fits you?

Ready to make your own list of hope-indicators?

Without being off-putting, tell how hopefulness describes your personality.

When I was a child, I spoke like a child, I thought like a child, I reasoned like a child; when I became an adult, I put an end to childish ways.
—1 Corinthians 13:11

If I hear the word "perky" again, I'll puke.[8]
—*Katie Couric (b. 1957), American television journalist*

135

63 Getting organized

If you're looking for a good model for hopeful actions, you might want to take a gander at community organizing. A consistent feature of overseas development efforts, community organizing is also an established way for people anywhere to take charge of their situation and solve seemingly intractable problems.

Hope lies at the base of community-organizing efforts—especially those based in congregations. Some features of community organizing might spark your hopeful actions.[9]

- Community organizing starts with intense appreciative conversations called "one-on-ones"
- One guiding principle—"Never do for others what they can do for themselves"—exemplifies the connection of self-reliance with hopeful expectations.
- Holding officials and leaders publicly accountable for keeping their promises and responsibly filling their roles ensures that community organizing accomplishes hopeful ends.
- Community organizers gather groups with diverse goals and help them develop a common identity and focused action. No one's hopes are dashed or disregarded.
- Every step in community organizing is founded on high respect for powerful people who are poor as well as powerful people who are not poor.

gritty, from Old English *greot,* "sand, dust, gravel" (The Lithuanian root *grudas* also denotes corn or other kernels.)

- Community organizers believe that there are no permanent friends and no eternal enemies.
- The hopeful work of community organizing is aimed at action, not just more conversation. Fueled by conversation, though, the planning process always results in a measurable goal or action.

You might spend some time with community-organizing efforts in your locale—they're spreading now from big cities to rural America, even into suburbs!—so that you apply the wisdom and gritty hope of community organizing to your own hopes.

You'll be happy you took this step.

What other organizational-development principles have been helpful to you?

Each of us was given grace according to the measure of Christ's gift.
—Ephesians 4:7

If you have come to help me, you are wasting your time. But if you have come because your liberation is bound up with mine, then let us work together.[10]
—*Lilla Watson (b. 1940), Australian Aboriginal activist*

64   No Santa Claus

Some purveyors of hope may want you to be constantly optimistic, forever insisting that all glasses are always half-full, and always smiling wistfully about possibilities. These folks might also want you to adopt Santa Claus and Pollyanna as your patron saints. (In *Bright-Sided*, social critic and cultural observer Barbara Erhenreich claims that the blind pursuit of happiness has distracted our good society and our good sense.)

So, as you begin or continue hopeful actions, you can free yourself from the clutches of a gooey hope that is judged more by its gosh-darn all-around niceness than by its ability to foster action. Consider any of these starter thoughts:

- When you're inspired to be hopeful, ask yourself the follow-up question, "Inspired to do what?"
- When you hear only platitudes about hopefulness, ask your word-server for a different menu.
- If you think hope is mostly about what's nice or kind, think again. Try this mind-set instead: What's good, righteous, or godly in what you're about to undertake?
- If hope is mostly magical—Santa Claus comes to mind again—remember that God's gifts come through rather ordinary means and rather ordinary people. Learn how to celebrate "ordinary."
- Don't let *glib* describe your hopeful speech, nor *shallow* characterize your hopeful actions.

glib, from Low German *glibberig,* "smooth or slippery" (probably from Middle Low German *glibber,* "jelly")

- When hopeful actions seem to require your understanding of complex Latinate cognates, doctrinal mechanics, or psychological wizardry, do something intuitively hopeful before you start the kind of complicated analysis that requires long sentences like this one.
- Always wonder who benefits from your acting hopefully. Insist that your actions don't perpetuate injustice or otherwise detract from the greater good.

You can stay hopeful and continue to act hopefully if you avoid the clutches of an empty search for happiness.

Or you could wait a long, long time for Santa.

When does your hopefulness become a practical way to approach life?

But be doers of the word, and not merely hearers who deceive themselves.
—James 1:22

A platitude is simply a truth repeated till people get tired of hearing it.[11]
—Stanley Baldwin (1867–1947),
British prime minister in 1920s and 1930s.

65   Like Harold's dog

Playing with words is a delightful activity. When it comes to matters of hopefulness, you might consider how hope-metaphors could enrich your identity as a person who does hopeful things. Metaphors and similes can be triggers for imagination, which is both a precursor to action and (mental) action itself. Play along with these possibilities:

- Insist on operational, action-driven definitions of hope and hope-related words. ("Hope happens when . . . " or "You can see hope because it . . .")
- Make up your own metaphors, and see how they might just work. ("Hope is like Harold's dog" or "Hope reminds me of a farmer reading the grain futures.")
- Eschew metaphorical mastication! (In other words, don't chew the metaphor into indigestable mush.)
- Play with the words, for heaven's sake. (Deep inside you is a God-given ability to put words and ideas into new containers, new combinations, new uses.)
- Try out your metaphors and similes on people who are not hopeful. (Think what you'll do after they ask, "What does that mean?")
- Put hope together with seemingly unrelated idea-partners. (What might happen if you combined hope with saliva,

metaphor, from the Greek *metaphora,* literally "a carrying over"

---

photography, the wind, the eyes of small children, or the time Harold's dog ate your Bible?)

- Don't be afraid of silly. (Hope's never silly, and metaphors grab hold of every part of your brain, a profound mental activity!)

As you use metaphors and similes to make hope lively and useful in your circles of influence, consider Jesus's use of this kind of thinking and teaching ("The kingdom of Heaven is like . . .") and its effects on those who heard his words. Although Jesus never knew about Harold's dog, he was able to bring hope to people in dire circumstances.

Just like the Savior he was!

What else might happen if you played with hopeful words?

A word in season, how good it is!
—Proverbs 15:23

You play best with the people you know.
—Anonymous

66 What are you hoping?

If "you are what you eat," then it stands to reason that "you are what you hope." In the case of food, its molecules transform the tissues of your body and brain. In the case of hope, its presence can change your outlook or identity. This entry provides some questions that can help you assess how hope may or may not be part of what your spirit consumes. The questions include the following:

- When, where, and with whom do you feel most hopeful? Why?
- Which of your hopes extend beyond your own self-interest, safety, or well-being?
- How long are you willing to wait for your hopes to be realized?
- What unhopeful ideals or behaviors are you still nibbling or devouring? (For example, whining, carping, finding fault, gossiping, or demonizing.)
- Which of your spiritual habits foster hope? Which take hope away from you or make you less apt to act hopefully?
- How much of your hope is short term, and how much long term? How do you connect those two points on your life's journey?
- Which among your hopes have always been part of your personality? Which are new to your life?

identity, from Latin *identitas,* "sameness," perhaps abstracted from phrase *idem et idem,* "over and over"

- With whom do you share your most cherished hopes? Your most cherished hopeful actions?
- Which of your hopes have been crushed, taken from you, rendered useless? What have you done about that?
- After which hope-hero do you try to pattern your life? How's that going?
- What secret hope would you like to tell someone else about?

One or more of your answers are likely to reveal how hope feeds your way of living, your identity, or your future. Perhaps you have already become what you hope!

Or perhaps you have to change your diet?

In what ways do you consume hope?

Better is the end of a thing than its beginning;
the patient in spirit are better than the proud in spirit.
—Ecclesiastes 7:8

Tell me what you eat, and I will tell you what you are.[12]
—Jean Anthelme Brillat-Savarin (1755–1826),
French lawyer and gastronome

67 Six conversation starters

Eventually you'll be talking about hope with people who are willing to listen and offer their own thoughts. To spread hope—a worthy action!—you will salt your conversations with hopeful matters. Here are six conversation starters, questions whose answers will uncover other topics for appreciative sharing. Use them as you wish; use them to spread hope into the lives of others.

- When do you experience hope?
- What's the source of your hope?
- What basic temperaments or actions characterize the hopeful people you know?
- In what ways is hope a skill that you possess?
- What stands in the way of your being hopeful?
- In what ways is hope a practical part of your life?
- For you, what's the opposite of hope?
- How do you keep hoping in these difficult times?
- How does hope spread, deepen, infuse, connect, meld, grow, increase, or seed other positive spiritual traits in you?
- How does your hope overwhelm or overcome other, less helpful ways of thinking?
- What follows hope? (What does it cause?)
- When has your hope surprised you or someone else?

start, from a polyglot European heritage, including original meanings such as "overthrow, hurl, pour out, rush, jerk suddenly, leap, fall headlong, gush out, move briskly" (In some dictionaries as many as thirty meanings!)

- When have you been tempted to give up hoping? What happened?
- How did you learn to be a hopeful person? (Who was your teacher?)

Someone you know probably thinks of you as a hopeful person, which makes your hope-sharings even more important. As you use any of the starters here—yes, there are more than six— you'll find yourself exploring other important matters, too. Once they've begun, these conversations may become the stuff from which good days are made.

Once they've started, these conversations may never stop.

With whom would you like to have your next hope-filled conversation?

Happy are those who find wisdom, and those who get understanding.
—Proverbs 3:13

Great conversation . . . requires an absolute running of two souls into one.[13]
*—Ralph Waldo Emerson (1803–1882),
American essayist, poet, philosopher*

68 Ten prayers for hopeful people

Prayers are actions, always. Prayers include physical and mental postures, the firing of neurons, overcoming inertia, conserving, resting, struggling internally, and connecting your interior and exterior life. These actions imply growth or change within you and engagement with others. Hopeful people like you pray actively!

Ten prayer starters follow here, ideas that might assist you to adjust your prayer life toward hopefulness. Adapt and expand these thoughts to make them your own.

Special courage: For bravery and integrity in the little places of life that collect together to become your entire approach to life.

Loneliness: To find hopeful others like you.

Scientists: That they remain undeterred in seeking answers to life's most vexing problems, especially the gathering darkness of ecological night.

Political leaders: For hardy souls and serving hearts, in the face of unjust criticism from selfish or small-minded constituents.

Repentance: That your sins slip from your soul, that you find words that can release you from shame and guilt. That you ask for forgiveness.

Discernment: To increase your skills of seeing and judging what's wise, useful, godly, and hopeful.

integrity, from Latin *integritatem,* "soundness, wholeness"

Willingness to forgive: That your spirit remain generous among people who are not hopeful, who disdain your hope, or who avoid any depth of thought.

New words: That you escape tattered verbiage and old ways of speaking and writing so that hope springs fresh in the minds of those who know you.

Generations to come: That you remain responsible to them and remain willing to learn from them.

Perseverance: That the work gloves of your hope keep your hands capable and willing to accomplish God's will without giving up.

May God continue to enliven your prayer life.

What would happen if you walked and prayed at the same time?

Pray without ceasing.
—1 Thessalonians 5:17

A man prayed, and at first he thought that prayer was talking. But he became more and more quiet until in the end he realized that prayer is listening.[14]
—Søren Kierkegaard

69 Profile: After the war

She's an older woman now, Barbara, slowing down but still actively hopeful. She lived through a major war that destroyed almost everything around her, but that also built up much of what's inside her.

Barbara was a small-town farm girl whose parents had themselves lost considerable wealth because of a previous war and afterward were forced to live very simply. But when Barbara married a wealthy industrialist from the big city, her fortunes reversed themselves. Soon thereafter the war came to their doorstep, and their growing family faced horrific events close at hand, enduring mind-numbing circumstance. After the war Barbara, her husband, and their children came to the United States as refugees. "In my life, I have gone from privation to luxury to poverty several times," she recounts, "and through it all I learned to accept my lot in life. I learned that there is always a new view beyond today's horizon. I learned to be hopeful, no matter what. There wasn't any other choice but to be satisfied."

You can learn how to act hopefully from the Barbaras in your locale. They may be veterans of wars, rural folk who are totally dependent on the weather, people just getting by, refugees who haven't forgotten where they came from, people who lived through the first Great Depression or who are living through this one now.

circumstance, from Latin *circumstare,* "stand around, surround"

It's good for you to learn from these people, to find yourself—your circumstances, your ideals, your hopefulness—in their stories. It's good to connect with Barbaras, wherever you find them, so that you don't ever forget that there are people all around you who have found their way through hellish circumstances and whose hopefulness has never diminished. If you know how to look, you might even see Christ in them.

Whatever their names and however old they are.

How will you act hopefully when you are faced with overwhelming adversity?

The LORD blessed the latter days of Job
more than his beginning.
—Job 42:12a

People who are in a fortunate position always attribute virtue to what makes them so happy.[15]
—*John Kenneth Galbraith, (1908–2006), Canadian-born American economist*

Part 6

Connections

70 You're *not* the only one

Your hope can grow like a happy field of dandelions when you understand and value your connectedness to others. Hopefulness depends on the presence of others to nourish and protect it. That's how its roots intertwine and grab hold in the soil of your identity. When that happens, hope can be difficult to pull loose. Despair also grows in its own weed field, but its ability to connect seems more sinister, as though all these weeds were feeding together on the same chemical fertilizer.

Because it's hard to hope, it makes sense that you value your hope-filled connections, whoever they are and wherever you can find them. These bonds with other like-minded people will surely sustain you through the coming years.

That's what you'll find in the entries that follow: "connectedness" as one way to think how hope clings to your soul with fierce tenacity. The entries tempt your imagination, asking you to think outside the boxed-in feeling that you're the only person working against despair's destruction of the human spirit. The entries also invite you to become a "connector," taking responsibility for being a hub, fiber, or power by which God's people are connected to the hope-giving of the Holy Spirit.

This section comes at the end of this field guide as a sign of the eventual triumph of hope, as though it will spread throughout the world like the victory of dandelions over grass, vivacious

connect, from the Latin *connectere,* "to fasten, bind, or tie together"

---

green-and-yellow plants sprouting puffball seeds and spreading them into every breeze or breath. Hope-weeds gone wild, covering despair's dullness with tenacious beauty!

May hope triumph in your life as well!

How wild and beautiful are your connections with other hopeful people?

And now faith, hope, and love abide, these three;
and the greatest of these is love.
—1 Corinthians 13:13

Sursum corda! (translation: Lift up your hearts!)
—from the Liturgy for Holy Communion

71   Think on these things

Philippians 4:8–9 is one of the most hopeful invitations contained in Scripture. In the Contemporary English Version (CEV), "think" becomes "keep your mind on," a much richer concept and action that connects hope to almost any other human endeavor or attribute. Although he writes from prison, Paul is hopeful because he is intimately and joyfully connected to his readers. He has begun his letter writing with thanks for these generous people (1:3), counted as garbage what is not important (3:7–9a), and enjoined them to rejoice (4:4). Thus gratitude, discernment, and joyfulness join the list of ideals Paul fastens together in this letter.

In this passage, Paul invites his readers to connect in their minds whatever is true, pure, right, holy, friendly, and proper. Manifestly important individually, together these qualities of the Christlike life describe mindful believers. In turn, each quality serves as a hub for its own connections (for example, what is "right" is probably also just and serves as a standard for life; what is "holy" could also be godly, set aside for sacred purposes).

Mindfulness connects to hopefulness because it describes the activity of a whole brain, with its interconnected structures, intensely attentive and focused on the matter at hand. Because Paul introduces this text with "finally," he implies that mindfulness is a summary or foundational trait of Christ's followers.

think, from a variety of lingual sources, including the Old English root verb *pyncan,* perhaps "cause to appear to oneself"

What finally connects all these ideals is hope. Without hope, mindfulness could tend towards despair, putting what is true, pure, right, holy, friendly, and proper into tiny, out-of-the-way places in the brains of people more highly inclined to fight, flee, or freeze. With hope in place, each quality that Paul upholds becomes powerful in itself and capable of energizing your entire spirit toward fulfilling God's will for the world.

A good place to connect all your mindfulnesses!

What other mindful hope-connectors might Paul have included?

Where your treasure is, there your heart will be also.
—Luke 12:34

Keeping your mind on anything is either a habit or hard work.
—Anonymous

72 Immunity everywhere

Involved in hopeful actions, you're part of a worldwide system that accomplishes God's will. Think of it as an immunity system. In that way of thinking, it's a living, remembering, learning, and self-regulating system that does more than just destroy invading germs.

Immunologists now recognize that your immune system is the most diverse and widespread network of your body. Almost like another mind, your immune system helps every part of you connect and communicate for the welfare of your entire body.

As a hopeful person, you are part of a global immunity system. So says Paul Hawken in *Blessed Unrest*. He imagines the present systems of global economics and politics as a disease that will certainly lead to the death of most of the planet's other systems. In his mind, people who act hopefully for the good of others are part of a powerful system that identifies what is not life-affirming and then contains, neutralizes, or eliminates that disease. Hawken suggests that this immune system is able to recognize what is humane and what is not. Acting much like an organism, the system is strong not because it knows how to fight but because it knows how to connect its workers.

The metaphor might be helpful at those moments when you're thinking that you're just a tiny speck in the larger immunity system, trying to do God's work despite your

disease, from Old French *desaise,* "without ease"

---

imagined lowly estate. Even if, in your humility, you don't use biological language, you probably get those feelings. "I'm too small to change the world; I'm too weak to defeat evil; I'm too insignificant to lead others." Because you're part of the vast collection of people working against evil, though, you can think differently: you're part of something big, powerful, interconnected, and undefeatable.

Ever thought of becoming a lymphocyte for God's purposes?

What else do you know about the power of your immunity system?

I am not asking you to take them out of the world, but I ask
you to protect them from the evil one.
—John 17:15

Love is the most powerful known stimulant to the immune system.[1]
—*Bernie Siegel (b. 20th century), physician and author*

73 Movements in the church

As a hopeful one, you're already connected to hopeful movements in the church, perhaps some like these:

New monastics. These thirty-something evangelicals are learning how to live joyfully with less. Sometimes living in intentional communities, they're insistent on economic justice, aware of the world around them, and fully engaged in changing the world. Their ego needs seem to be low, sometimes making them as hard to find as hermits. Even though they aren't.

Emergent churches. This already-overused phrase describes a way of doing church that is as radical and diverse as first-century congregational life. Simplicity characterizes worship, congregational structures, and the roles of pastor and leaders. Reminiscent of house churches, emergent congregations seem humble about their identity and the directions in which they are headed. They seem viable over the long haul.

New evangelicals. This movement seems well connected to the Jesus of Scripture. This subgroup within evangelical Christianity is engaged and engaging, diverse and aware. Respectful of their roots, these evangelicals are now challenging the sometimes dispirited directions of their spiritual forefathers. They welcome ecumenical partners as well.

Liturgical renewal. This hopeful form of renewal takes maturing congregations past worship practices that are noisy, ego-burdened, and entertainment-infested. Respectful of past, present,

hierarchy, from Greek *hierarches,* "high priest, leader of sacred rites"

---

and future, leaders in this movement now embrace new styles and voices, especially those of other cultures.

Denominational decline. The deterioration of the institutional church is hopeful when its leaders repent, when purpose and meaning are distilled and focused toward bedrock principles and in sustainable directions. Denominational decline might be hopeful when hierarchical models of governance are replaced by the disciplines of servanthood, or when parachurch enterprises grow into new, thriving associations.

However you name them, and wherever you are connected, you can be glad that God's Spirit is moving hopefully within the church.

Perhaps even within a church near you.

What hopeful movements do you notice occurring in your part of the body of Christ?

Now you are the body of Christ and individually members
of it.
—1 Corinthians 12:27

*A Christian . . . is the most free lord of all, and subject to none;
a Christian . . .is the most dutiful servant of all, and subject to every one.*[2]
—*Martin Luther*

74   A congregation named Hope

Some of the liveliest hope-connections you can find are within your own congregation. In this entry you meet a make-believe congregation whose name is Hope, as is its way of conducting God's business. This description might help you see how to find hopeful connections within your congregation. At Hope Church:

- The pastor works as a bivocational leader so that she keeps her connections with the worlds in which congregation members live hopefully.
- Planning starts with an assessment of the useful gifts of leaders and members, assets available for mission.
- Leaders know each other's faith journeys, especially the difficult parts.
- The mission statement is adjusted to fit the results of each leadership change and each assessment of useful gifts.
- Most of the congregation's programs help members cope with lifestyle matters. (*Stewardship* is a big word at Hope.)
- Whiners aren't given much attention. Honest disagreements flourish, though, and so do respectful compromises.
- Youth and adult education is combined so that both groups can teach and learn from each other about their common interest in the past, present, and future.
- Teen mission trips equip participants with useful life skills.
- The prayer life of the congregation—in worship and beyond—includes matters of the world community.

congregation, from Latin *congregare,*
"to collect into a flock, gather"

- The congregation has requested a seminary intern from another country.
- Several congregational leaders are trained in the arts of community organizing.
- Several women offer ongoing programs—gardening, sewing, computer skills, English as a second language—that benefit a group of sponsored refugees who have become part of Hope.
- Entrepreneurial leadership has gradually supplanted the model of elected leaders and appointed committees.

Hope Church members and leaders act on the strength of their hopes and have found deep satisfaction in this approach.

Perhaps you will, too.

What signs of hope can you name in your congregation?

After this I looked, and there was a great multitude that no one could count, from every nation, from all tribes and peoples and languages, standing before the throne and before the Lamb.
—Revelation 7:9

The Church is not a gallery for the exhibition of eminent Christians, but a school for the education of imperfect ones.[3]
—*Henry Ward Beecher (1813–1887), American pastor and abolitionist*

75   Coalescence unearthed

Although there are many ways to think about how hope connects to other important matters, the concept (and practice) of "coalescence" affords some fresh possibilities. This word's meanings denote a fusing or growing together, perhaps a stronger connection than *unified* or *collected*. As proposed in Paul Hawken's *Blessed Unrest*, this term could help you understand *hopeful connections* in these ways:

- It implies aggregation. Hope gathers, in powerful ways, a vast collection of attributes, possibilities, people, and helpful attitudes.
- Coalescence suggests inextricable bonding. Hope bonds people together, fostering identity, emotions, and actions that maintain their wholeness over time.
- The bonding power of hope might also be thought of as a magnetic force, a "stickiness of energy" that brings hopeful people and ideas together.
- Because the coalescence eventually results in something large (and perhaps lively), its sheer size leads to movement, if only because of gravity. As it moves, the large sticky thing grabs hold of other things. (Yes, hope can grab hold!)
- As things move, problems are resolved. The small theological principle *solvitur ambulando*—"The matter will resolve

organic, from Greek *organikus,* "of or pertaining to an organ (instrument)"

---

itself as it moves along"—suggests that movement can be ultimately hopeful.

- When it comes to large-scale movements—of history, civilizations, or spirit—coalescence implies a fierce tenacity by which hopeful people are held together for common purposes. Think of the Protestant Reformation, the emergence of Pentecostal strands of Christianity, or the long standing traditions of lay leadership excellence.

When hopeful people gather together, their work is self-organizing, indivisible, many-sided, frangible, not easily described—all necessary for a movement that will change the world.

So, now are you ready to coalesce with other lively, hopeful people?

What would happen if you thought of yourself glued to a large, hopeful movement?

Then I looked, and I heard the voice of many angels surrounding the throne and the living creatures and the elders; they numbered myriads and thousands of thousands.
—Revelation 5:11

A metaphor for coalescence: You're surrounded!

76   Profile: Down but not out

To maintain his dignity we'll call him "a person who is homeless." His name is Josh, and he's been homeless for about ten weeks now. His lifestyle is a migration among a set of nightly shelters strung out along commuter train lines. He thinks of himself less as homeless and more as a writer. Why? Josh is a writer of inspirational literature, poetry, and motivational messages that he posts on his website.

What's hopeful about Josh? First, he's not a complainer. Second, he's smart about "being homeless," already sorting out the folks who have chosen permanent life on the streets from those who will eventually claw their way out of their situation. Third, Josh is gathering notes for a book about homelessness, written from the inside. He says that it will be a tell-all, but also "inspiring and hopeful."

Josh is also a connector. He has been thinking about the way to solve homelessness. It has to do with jobs. Josh is working to set up a nonprofit called HELP, which will connect the skills of homeless folks with people needing odd jobs, routine maintenance, and other services in the suburbs that ring his large metropolitan area. In his weeks in homeless programs, he's seen people with those skills, and before he lost his home he knew firsthand about the small jobs that many suburbanites can't or won't tackle. He sees a niche market there.

home, from Old High German *heim,* the Old Frisian *hem,* the Old Saxon *hēm,* the Old English *hām,* the Dutch *heem,* and the Old Norse *heimr,* all of which indicate "village" or "home"

Josh is not alone. If you'd talk to other shelter guests, you'd find many who are down but are definitely not out. They're connected to each other, to those who want to be helpful, to organizations that are both smart and helpful. They won't stay where they are for long. Josh will see to that.

Perhaps the most dignified way to describe Josh is "a person who is hopeful."

**What would it take for you to be hopeful if you had
nowhere to call home?**

Foxes have holes, and birds of the air have nests; but the Son
of Man has nowhere to lay his head.
—Matthew 8:20

We may be homeless, but we're not helpless.[4]
—Ricky J. Fico, homeless advocate

Afterword

It's not too late. If it were too late—for hope or any other godly attribute—you'd have chosen to read a different book. That field guide might have been about surviving some well-documented problem in society, beating the odds, or getting away from the maddening crowd.

But that's not what you decided to do. Instead, you just finished reading—and are starting to use—a hope-filled book that may guide your thoughts and actions for the foreseeable future. You began this book with full knowledge of the deep difficulties that the world faces in the coming years. But you're still willing to proclaim in your actions a lively, practical hope that can undergird your basic mind-set in the coming days. You have chosen hope over despair.

What comes next will be the joyful-yet-difficult task of sticking with this matter of hopeful living, on your own as well as in the company of other hopeful people. Remember that despair doesn't give up easily. It may be a preferred attitude in your brain. The problems of these times will sorely tempt you to give in to sodden fear and the desperations of individualism.

But hope is always practical, always useful, always effective. For that reason, and because God's powerful promises never go unfulfilled, keep at what you've learned here. Share what you've learned with someone you trust—and then share those thoughts

accompany, from Old French *acompaignier*, "take as a companion"

---

again with someone you don't know. Fill your mind and your words with what is hopeful, and let hope guide your decisions, no matter their size. When the times seem most difficult, revisit this guide to remind yourself and others about how and where to find hope. Continue to fill your prayers with gratitude and your actions with generosity.

May God accompany you along the way.

What's next for you?

No one who puts a hand to the plow and looks back is fit
for the kingdom of God.
—Luke 9:62

*God has two dwellings; one in heaven, and the other in a meek and
thankful heart.*[1]
*—Izaak Walton (1593–1683),
English writer, the "father of angling"*

Notes

Preface

1. Fragment on free labor, Sept. 17, 1859? *Collected Works of Abraham Lincoln*, vol. 3 (New Brunswick, N.J.: Rutgers University Press, 1953, 1990), 462.

2. Booker T. Washington, address, Sept. 18, 1895, Atlanta Exposition; included in his *Up From Slavery* (New York: Doubleday, 1901).

3. José Ortega y Gasset, "To the Reader," *Meditations on Quixote* (1914), trans. from the Spanish by Evelin Rugg and Diego Martin (Urbana, Ill.: University of Illinois Press, 2000).

Contexts

1. Robert Frost, "Sand Dunes," *Complete Poems of Robert Frost* (New York: Holt, Rinehart, and Winston, 1949, 1962).

2. E-mail message from Norm Brockmeier, chemical engineer and president, Oakwood Consulting, Inc., Wheaton, Ill., Sept. 23, 2009.

3. Arnold Joseph Toynbee and David Churchill Somervell, *A Study of History: Abridgement of Volumes VII-X*, vol. 2 (Oxford, U.K.: Oxford University Press, 1957), 350.

4. Alexander Dumas, *The Count of Monte Cristo*, vol. 2 of 2, (Forgotten Books, 2008).

5. Malcolm X, as quoted in Charles G. Hurst, Jr., "Malcolm X: A Community with a New Perspective," *Black World/Negro Digest,* vol. XIX, no. 5 (March 1970): 36.

6. Jane Addams, quoted in Editors of Reader's Digest, *Quotable Quotes* (Pleasantville, N.Y.: Reader's Digest Association, 1997), 72.

Openings

1. John Ashbery, "Unctuous Platitudes," in *Collected Poems 1956–1987* (New York: Penguin Group, 2008), 498.

2. David Heim, sermon at Faith Lutheran Church, Glen Ellyn, Ill., Dec. 2008.

3. Woodrow Wilson, *The Atlantic Monthly,* August 1921.

4. Andrew Newberg, Eugene D'Aquili, and Vince Rause, *Why God Won't Go Away: Brain Science and the Biology of Belief* (New York: Ballantine Books, 2001).

5. Søren Kierkegaard, "Balance Between Esthetic and Ethical," *Either/Or,* vol. 2 (1843, trans. 1987).

6. Václav Havel, *Disturbing the Peace* (New York: Vintage Books, 1990), 181.

7. D. Lyman, *The Moral Sayings of Publius Syrus: A Roman Slave* (Cleveland: L.E. Barnard & Company, 1856), 68.

8. Dan Ariely, *Predictably Irrational: The Hidden Forces that Shape our Decisions* (New York: Harper Collins, 2008), 86ff.

9. Friedrich Nietzsche, *Sämtliche Werke: Kritische Studienausgabe, vol. 2,* eds. Giorgio Colli and Mazzino Montinari (Berlin: Walter de Gruyter, 1980), 323.

10. Friedrich Nietsche, *Sämtliche Werke, vol. 3, The Gay Science,* first edition, "Third Book," aphorism 130, "A Dangerous Resolution" (1882), 485.

11. Muriel Rukeyser, "To Enter that Rhythm Where the Self Is Lost," *Waterlily Fire: Poems 1935–1962* (New York: Macmillan, 1962).

12. Hubert H. Humphrey, speech at White House Conference on International Cooperation, Nov. 29, 1965.

Bogs

1. Al Capone's gravestone can be found at Mount Carmel Cemetery in Chicago (see http://en.wikiquote.org/wiki/Epitaphs).

2. Satan, in John Milton, *Paradise Lost,* bk. 1, 190–191 (1667).

3. Martin Luther, *The Table Talk of Martin Luther*, trans. and ed. William Hazlitt (London: Bell & Daldy, 1872), 146.

4. Albert Einstein, written statement (Sept. 1937), quoted in Helen Dukas and Banesh Hoffman, eds., *Albert Einstein, The Human Side: New Glimpses From His Archives* (Princeton, N.J.: Princeton University Press, 1979).

5. Thorstein Veblen, *An Inquiry Into the Nature of Peace, and the Terms of Its Perpetuation* (New York: Macmillan, 1917), 168.

6. Victor Hugo, *Les Misérables* (New York: Random House, Modern Library edition, 1992), 643.

7. Epictetus, *Enchiridion*, part XLII, in *The Moral Discourses of Epictetus*, trans. Elizabeth Carter (London: J. M. Dent Sons, 1910), 270.

8. Lester R. Brown, address at Fortune Brainstorm Conference, Aspen, Colo., 2006.

Skills

1. Tony Tyznik, conversation with the author, May 2009.

2. Søren Kierkegaard, quoted in Howard V. Hong, *The Sickness Unto Death: A Christian Psychological Exposition for Upbuilding and Awakening*

(Princeton, N.J.: Princeton University Press, 1980), 18.

3. Mother Teresa, *A Gift for God: Prayers and Meditations* (New York: HarperCollins, 1996), 44.

4. Indira Gandhi, as quoted in People magazine, June 30, 1975.

5. Eleanor H. Porter, *Pollyanna: Complete and Unabridged* (orig. pub. in Great Britain: Harrap, 1927; reissued New York: Puffin, 1994).

6. Robert Frost, "Haec Fabula Docet," *Complete Poems of Robert Frost* (New York: Holt, Rinehart and Winston, 1949, 1962).

7. Woody Allen, multiple sources, including dishmag.com/issue84/celebrity/8350/dish-talks-to-woody-allen/

8. Jules Feiffer, quoted in *Webster's New World Dictionary of Quotations* (Edinburg, Scotland: Harrap Publishers Ltd., 2005).

9. Anne Lamott, *Bird by Bird: Some Instructions on Writing and Life* (New York: Pantheon Books, 1994), xxiii.

10. This quotation probably had its origin in Erich Maria Remarque's novel *Der schwarze Obelisk* (1956): "Aber das ist wohl so, weil ein einzelner immer der Tod ist—und zwei Millionen immer nur eine Statistik."

11. "Von" (last name withheld), conversation with the author, Apr. 13, 2009.

12. Of course this isn't *really* a survey—there's nothing statistically significant here. But your "score" is a place to start a conversation about your hopefulness skills. Enjoy the conversation!

13. Paul Hawken, *Blessed Unrest: How the Largest Social Movement in History Is Restoring Grace, Justice, and Beauty to the World* (New York: Penguin, 2007), 84.

Actions

1. Cited in http://en.wikiquote.org/wiki/Bhutanese_proverbs in section on "Wisdom/Insight."

2. Hawken, *Blessed Unrest*, 85.

3. As found on several Web sites, notably http://www.motherlandnigeria.com/proverbs.html

4. Variant of "A journey of a thousand miles begins with a single step." From *Tao Te Ching*. (See http://en.wikiquote.org/wiki/Chinese_proverbs; also attributed to Lao-tzu.)

5. George Washington Carver, "A Boy Who Was Traded for a Horse," *American Magazine*, vol. 114 (Oct. 1932): 25, 112.

6. Marian Wright Edelman, *The Measure of Our Success: A Letter to My Child and Yours* (Boston: Beacon Press, 1992), 71.

7. Johann Wolfgang von Goethe, letter to Carl Friedrich Zelter, Dec. 3, 1812 (see http://en.wikiquote.org/wiki/Goethe).

8. Katie Couric, quote from dustjacket of Jesse Shiers, *The Quotable Bitch: Women Who Tell it Like It Really Is* (Guilford, Ct.: Lyons Press, 2008). Also reported in *Huffington Post* (http://www.huffingtonpost.com/2008/08/25/katie-couric-hits-the-ham_n_121210.html?view=print).

9. For an easily accessible introduction to community organizing, see *Hope at Work* at www.elca.org/Our-Faith-In-Action/Justice/Congregation-based-Organizing/Comic-Book.aspx.

10. Lilla Watson, as cited on Web site for New York to New Orleans Coalition (NY2NO), http://current.com/items/89559099_ny2no-if-you-have-come-to-help-me.htm (watch embedded video, then scroll down to see citation).

11. Stanley Baldwin, speech to the British Parliament, *Hansard*, May 29, 1924.

12. Jean Anthelme Brillat-Savarin, as cited in Mary Elizabeth Braddon, *Belgravia*, vol. 26 (London: Warwick House, 1875), 402.

13. Ralph Waldo Emerson, "Friendship," in *Essays, First Series* (1841, reprinted 1847).

14. Consistently attributed to Søren Kierkegaard (see, for example, *The Experience of Prayer* by Terry W. Glaspey).

15. John Kenneth Galbraith, *The Guardian,* U.K., May 23, 1992.

Connections

1. Bernie Siegel, *Love, Medicine, & Miracles: Lessons Learned about Self-healing from a Surgeon's Experience with Exceptional Patients* (New York: Harper & Row, 1986), 181.

2. Martin Luther, as cited in *First Principle of the Reformation*, trans. and notated Henry Wace, Karl Adolph Buchheim, and Robert Scarlett Grignon (London: John Murray, 1883), 104.

3. Henry Ward Beecher and Edna Dean Proctor, *Life Thoughts: Gathered from the Extemporaneous Discourses of Henry Ward Beecher* (New York: Sheldon & Company, 1860), 259.

4. Conversation with the author at a homeless shelter in Glen Ellyn, Illinois, summer 2008.

Afterword

1. Izaak Walton, *The Compleat Angler*, as cited in *Chambers Cyclopedia of English Literature,* vol. 1, p. 617.

Bibliography

The following books—some with accompanying websites—may be helpful in your further exploration of hopeful living. Some of these volumes can also serve as alarm clocks for "the times to come," and thus add a sense of urgency to your hope-seeking. Enjoy what you read!

Ariely, Dan. *Predictably Irrational: The Hidden Forces that Shape Our Decisions.* New York: HarperCollins, 2008.

> Quirky at first glance, Ariel's book is filled with hope, because it opens our eyes to the actual decision-making processes that occur in our society.

Brown, Lester R. *Plan B 3.0: Mobilizing to Save Civilization.* New York: W.W. Norton & Company, 2008.

> Eminent researcher and social commentator Lester Brown presents a both sobering and hopeful assessment of the decline of the earth's capacity to sustain life. (Note: The entire book is available for download at *www.earth-policy.org*. Check, too, to see whether a newer edition is now available.)

Diamond, Jared. *Collapse: How Societies Choose to Fail or Succeed.* New York: Penguin Books, 2005.

> One of the original end-of-the-world-as-we-know-it books, this volume by Pulitzer Prize–winning Jared Diamond presents striking examples throughout history of the fate of societies in

which individualism prevented a greater wisdom from taking hold. (For a user's guide, see *http://us.penguingroup.com/static/rguides/us/collapse.html*.)

Friend, Howard E., Jr. *Gifts of an Uncommon Life: The Practice of Contemplative Activism*. Herndon, Va.: Alban Institute, 2009.

> Parish pastor, author, and consultant Howard Friend turns his inward thoughts outward, offering readers an alternative approach to changing the world. Hopeful in its quiet storytelling, the book invites readers' own calm in the middle of society's rushings about.

Gladwell, Malcolm. *Outliers: The Story of Success*. New York: Little, Brown and Company, 2008.

> The author of the now-classic *Tipping Point* spells out his theory of why people are successful. His conclusions, although somewhat surprising, seem to offer hope about the effects of small details on the elusive matter of "success in life."

Haueisen, Kathryn, and Carol H. Flores. *A Ready Hope: Effective Disaster Ministry for Congregations*. Herndon, Va.: Alban Institute, 2009.

> Ostensibly a how-to manual for congregations that are wisely preparing for their ministries in disaster relief, this book also offers to any congregational leader help in finding the hopeful attitudes and skills that are helpful in any mind-numbing difficulty.

Hawken, Paul. *Blessed Unrest: How the Largest Social Movement in History Is Restoring Grace, Justice, and Beauty to the World*. New York: Penguin Books, 2007.

> The subtitle describes this delightful book completely but does not mention Hawken's amazing appendix, which categorizes the literal multitude of enterprises comprising the "movement" Hawken details. (Also see *www.blessedunrest.com*.)

McKibben, Bill. *Deep Economy: The Wealth of Communities and the Durable Future*. Oxford, U.K.: Oneworld Publications, 2007.

> A compelling read by a behavioral economist, this work details how "hyper-individualism" makes more vulnerable a world intended for communitarian behaviors. (Also see *www.billmckibben. com/deep-economy.html*.)

Musil, Robert K. *Hope for a Healed Planet: How Americans Are Fighting Global Warning and Building a Better Future*. New Brunswick, N.J.: Rutgers University Press, 2009.

> In this approachable and personal testimony the author, an American University scholar and past president of Physicians for Social Responsibility, lays out a convincing case for hope about global warning. A measured and faith-filled tone makes the book readable and actionable. Musil is thorough, fair, and honest in his writing. A man of faith and intellect, he is compelling in his logic and persuasive in his invitation.

Patnaik, Dev. *Wired to Care: How Companies Prosper When They Create Widespread Empathy*. San Mateo, Calif.: Jump Associates, 2009.

> Consultant and university teacher Dev Patnaik spins tales of companies that take seriously the matter of empathy—one of hope's correlates?—as their basic framework for doing business.

Ratey, John. *Spark: The Revolutionary New Science of Exercise and the Brain*. New York: Little, Brown, 2008.

> One of the most hopeful books I've read in years, this volume shows how the simple human activity of exercise can literally change the worlds inside and around us. Scientifically grounded and oriented toward hope-filled living.

Roberts, Paul. *The End of Food.* Boston: Houghton Mifflin, 2008.

Author of *The End of Oil* opens the lid on the vulnerability of present-day food production and distribution systems worldwide. A sobering look at a way of living that will likely come apart.

Swedish, Margaret. *Living Beyond the 'End of the World': A Spirituality of Hope.* Maryknoll, N.Y.: Orbis, 2008.

Popular speaker and blogger Margaret Swedish continues her warnings and invitations for global change in this incisive treatment of hope. Of special interest are her thoughts about the problems that have come from religion itself! (See also *www. ecologicalhope.org.*)

Williams, Cassandra D. Carkuff. *Learning the Way: Reclaiming Wisdom from the Earliest Christian Communities.* Herndon, Va.: Alban Institute, 2009.

American Baptist executive Cassandra Williams takes readers back into the first centuries of church life, helping unearth and proclaim approaches to congregational life and individual faithfulness that have stood the test of time. Williams's work here serves as a history lesson about hope in difficult times.